MASTERING MIXED MARTIAL ARTS
THE GUARD

ANTONIO RODRIGO NOGUEIRA

with GLEN CORDOZA & ERICH KRAUSS

Las Vegas, Nevada

First Published in 2008 by Victory Belt Publishing.

Copyright © 2007 Antonio Rodrigo Nogueira, Erich Krauss & Glen Cordoza

ISBN 10: 0-9815044-2-6
ISBN 13: 978-0-9815044-2-1

This book is for educational purposes. The publisher and authors of this instructional book are not responsible in any manner whatsoever for any adverse effects arising directly or indirectly as a result of the information provided in this book. If not practiced safely and with caution, martial arts can be dangerous to you and to others. It is important to consult with a professional martial arts instructor before beginning training. It is also very important to consult with a physician prior to training due to the intense and strenuous nature of the techniques in this book.

Cover Design by Michael J. Morales, VIP GEAR
Cover Photos by Brian Rule
Printed in Hong Kong

CONTENTS

∽POSTURE CONTROL∾

CLOSED GUARD POSTURE CONTROL

SITTING-UP GUARD POSTURE CONTROL

OPEN GUARD POSTURE CONTROL

DOUBLE ARM CONTROLS

INSIDE HOOKS GUARD

HALF GUARD

SINGLE HOOK CONTROL

CROSS-FACE AND HIP BLOCK CONTROL

HALF GUARD TROUBLESHOOTING

❧DOWNED GUARD☙

There are two things I've always been able to count on: my family and the martial arts. And they have always been connected.

I spent my early years in a farmhouse located in the sprawling countryside of northeast Brazil. At first my parents just had my two brothers, two sisters, and me, but when my mother's sister passed away, my folks brought her four children in with loving warmth. As one might imagine, it was difficult for them to manage nine kids, so every afternoon when my mother went to the fitness club she owned, she brought us youngsters with her.

The gym offered all kinds of martial arts classes. They had judo, tae kwon do, karate, and some type of crazy kung fu. With nothing else to do, I went to all of them. In the beginning my attendance was mainly just a way to pass the time, but then my older brother began competing in judo. My twin brother, Rogerio, and I would always go check out his matches to cheer him on. Unfortunately, not much cheering could be done. Despite being a good judo player in training, our older brother didn't fare so well in the tournaments, due to his nerves. Rogerio and I were just four years old at the time, but apparently we didn't take to our brother's losses, because we both began training judo more seriously. A short while later, we started competing and winning.

From the beginning, Rogerio has been my best training partner. We were the same size and weight. We had the same strength, the same heart. If I was having a bad day, he would push me, and if he had a bad day, I gave him the encouragement he needed. We grew together as martial artists. Unlike a lot of brothers, there was very little competition between us. We'd tear into each other to improve our skills, but never to see which one of us was the best. This included the times when we both made it to the finals of a tournament. Before we had to fight each other, we'd go to our father. He would turn to one of us and say, "This time you give the medal to your brother." Sometimes Rogerio would fight so I won, and other times I would fight so he won. We were kids, so it wasn't like we were throwing a fight. We were protecting our family bond, and proud to do so.

In addition to encouraging our involvement in the martial arts and competition, my parents also kept all of their kids on a healthy diet and workout regime. As a result, I became really in tune with my body and what it could do. I derived pleasure from testing my mental and physical limitations. Little did I know that the biggest test I would ever face was not waiting for me twenty or thirty years down the road, but rather just around the corner.

One afternoon when I was eleven, my family went to my cousin's house for a birthday party. As usual, all of us kids were running around outside, playing silly games. At some point, we all convened behind a truck parked in the driveway. I don't recall what we were doing, but I remember the truck starting up. The driver had been drinking, and he backed up extremely fast. Rogerio dove for safety and tried to pull me with him, but his grip slipped. All I could do was get my head out of the way before the truck ran over me. The tires crushed my torso and legs. Unconscious and bleeding profusely, my family rushed me to the hospital.

Although I was in a coma with machines pumping oxygen into my lungs, I could hear people around me talking. I could hear the doctors telling my family that my chances of making it were slim. I had lost a large portion of my liver, and my lungs were damaged severely. Luckily, I had the support of my family. I could always hear my grandmother in the room, praying for me, and it gave me the motivation I needed to fight. When I finally came to, I still needed a machine to breathe, but I knew that I would survive.

It was a long road to recovery. I developed an infection in my lungs due to my crushed diaphragm, and I also developed several infections from the hospital. I needed special attention, so my family took me to the city of Salvador, which had the best hospital in the area. I stayed in the hospital room for ten months, learning how to breathe and walk again. To support me

during the recovery phase, my family moved to Salvador part-time. As it turned out, we didn't leave. My mother and father's relationship was coming to an end, so my mother moved to Salvador to start fresh. I stayed with her, slowly rehabbing my body through swimming and lifting light weights.

The doctors had said that I would never again be involved in the martial arts, but I was determined to prove them wrong. By thirteen, my body not only felt back to normal, but I also felt mentally stronger. As soon as I got my mother's permission, I began searching for a boxing gym. I was interested in learning the sport for two reasons. The first reason is because some of my biggest idols growing up were boxers. I was a big fan of Mike Tyson because he always looked for the knockout, and I admired Evander Holyfield for his toughness in the ring and the quiet, humble life he led outside of it. But the boxer I looked up to most was Luis Dorea, a junior world champion boxer who hailed from the same state of Brazil as me. It seemed like every time I turned on the TV, there he was, knocking his opponent out. He was an American champion, a Brazilian champion, one of the top six best fighters in the world in his weight class, and a hero to millions of kids like me in Brazil. I figured that if I could follow in his footsteps, my life would be complete.

The second reason I wanted to take up boxing had to do with protecting myself. The city in which I went to school was littered with street gangs, and on a regular basis those gangs would come to the playgrounds to beat up us younger kids. At the time, I had done a good deal of martial arts training, but I knew enough about fighting to realize that kung fu doesn't work all that well on the street. I didn't want to be forced to drop my head and let these thugs do whatever they wanted to me—I wanted to be able to fight back and protect myself, and studying boxing seemed like the quickest route to achieve that goal.

As it turned out, I didn't have to go far to get the instruction I needed. Once on the hunt, I discovered a boxing gym just down the street from my house in Salvador. I probably would have kept looking just to see what else was out there, but when I walked into the place, I saw my boxing idol, Luis Dorea. He wasn't in a framed picture pinned to the wall or on the TV—he was standing there in the flesh, giving instructions to a student. A few minutes later, I found out it was his gym, and he was willing to become my official boxing coach. It was a huge honor for me, and still is today. Whenever I fight abroad, I bring Dorea with me. When it comes to striking, he is one of the best coaches around.

I saw boxing as a way to protect myself and stay in shape, but at the time I didn't have a huge urge to compete in it. Although I'd take a fight here and there, I wanted to be involved in a martial art I felt extremely passionate about. I decided to give jiu-jitsu a try, and it clicked with me immediately. The positions and submissions just came naturally, as if my body were built for the sport.

A part of my early success in jiu-jitsu had to do with talent, but an even larger part had to do with my instructor, Gierasad, a Carlson Gracie student who had earned his black belt from the De La Riva Academy. He was extremely technical, always focusing on the details, such as my grips. Over the years I had been to a lot of jiu-jitsu academies, watching how various instructors acted and taught, so I knew just how lucky I was. Gierasad was an amazing man both in and out of the academy.

Just as with judo, my brother proved to be my best training partner in both jiu-jitsu and boxing. He advanced just as quickly, and soon we knew all of each other's tricks. It became impossible to catch one another in a submission, but it was never due to a lack of trying. In the thousands of battles I've had in the gym, the top ten hardest ones have been with my brother. We pushed each other constantly, and he kept me on a good diet. I can honestly say that I would not have made it this far if I didn't have my bother by my side, pushing me every step of the way.

Once I had a solid jiu-jitsu foundation, I began competing. I did very well right out of the gate, winning the majority of tournaments that I entered. In no time at all, jiu-jitsu became my life. I practically lived in the academy. Not interested in doing anything else, I began teaching jiu-jitsu at seventeen. I didn't make enough to support myself, but thankfully my father believed in me and my talents and helped supplement my income. I wasn't sure what my training would lead to, but that wasn't important at the time. My only goal was to improve upon my skills and become the best jiu-jitsu player I could be.

Being a part of Carlson Gracie's team, we would travel to Rio de Janeiro to train at the main Academy. At that point, I had done very little no-gi grappling, but at the Carlson Gracie Academy they grappled three times a week without a gi. I immediately liked it. When you grapple with a gi, your opponent can stifle your movement by latching on to your uniform, but that's much harder to accomplish when you grapple without a gi. I was able to employ my hips, use the movements my opponents had always been able to control, and I did quite well. I would have continued to train without a gi in Rio, but my mother had decided to move to Miami, Florida, and I moved with her.

Having spent several years developing my game and training with a variety of people at a number of places, I finally knew what I wanted to do with the skills I had acquired—I wanted to become a professional fighter. I knew it would be a long road. This was back in 1999, long before the mixed martial arts explosion. The sport had some fans, but it also had a lot of enemies. It was uncertain as to what the future had in store for MMA, but that didn't matter to me. I had found my calling, and I was going to follow it.

As with many things in my life, I couldn't have done it without the support of my family. When I came to America, I couldn't speak a word of English, which pretty much ruled out the possibility of getting a job. Even though I had been training many years without any financial reward, my parents still believed in me, and they paid for my living expenses. To get the no-gi training I needed to compete, I began practicing with Marcus Silveira and several of his guys. At the time, he was getting ready to compete in an MMA fighting tournament. After we had trained several times, he approached me with an offer.

"They have one heavyweight, and no one wants to fight him," he said. "He's like 12 and 0, but I think you can beat him. You have better

boxing than this guy, and you're better on the ground. You should give it a try."

I trained for six months for the fight. The purse wasn't large enough to even pay for a week's worth of food, but that didn't matter. I was twenty years old and wanted to kick-start my career. I would have fought every weekend for free if that's what it took.

So, in June 1999 I drove over to Tommy Lawrence Arena in Deland, Florida, and took on David Dodd in the World Extreme Fighting 6. It turned out to be a fairly good fight. He threw me a couple of times from the standing position and I executed a number of the half guard sweeps that you'll find in this book. It went back and forth, but before the end of the first round, I secured side control, locked him in the crucifix position, and applied a choke that forced him to tap.

Four months later I fought in World Extreme Fighting 7, and again submitted my opponent. I had heard that RINGS, an MMA organization based out of Japan, was looking for two heavyweight fighters for their upcoming King of Kings tournament. It was the most prestigious tournament around at the time, which meant that not only would the competitors be more challenging, but the prize money would also be more rewarding. I knew I didn't have a very impressive resume, but I sent it to them nonetheless, just to see what happened.

As it turned out, more than two hundred heavyweights had had the same idea as me and sent their pictures and tapes to RINGS, all of which wound up on the desk of Akira Maeda, the head of the organization. After looking through all two hundred submissions, he pulled two aside and handed them to the promoter.

"You have to call these two fighters today," he said.

The promoter looked at the names of the fighters, and then shook his head. "Most of the fighters in those files have twenty or thirty fights. These two guys . . . one guy has two fights, and the other guy has three fights. Why them?"

"I know fighters," Maeda said. "I want these two guys, they're going to be good. Trust me. I want you to call them today."

The two files belonged to Fedor Emelianenko and me.

Twenty days after my last fight in World Extreme Fighting, I was standing in a ring in Japan surrounded by thousands of mixed martial arts fans. Unlike my previous fights, this was a tournament, which meant I had a second fight ahead of me if my first fight went well. Although I was seriously lacking in experience, my jiu-jitsu came to my rescue and I defeated my first opponent with an armbar and my second opponent with an Americana. It was a nice accomplishment, but not the end of the road. In order to win the tournament, I had to return in four months and fight two more times against those who had won on the opposite side of the bracket. One of those competitors was amateur wrestler and future PRIDE superstar Dan Henderson.

In order to properly train for a fight, you have to push yourself beyond your limits every day in training. I wasn't able to do that in Florida. The two brown belts I worked out with gave me their all, but I needed to be grappling with world champions. Frustrated, I talked with Ricardo Liborio at the Carlson Gracie Academy back in Brazil. He told me to come

down, that he would find me some sponsorship money and, more importantly, some people to train with. I took him up on his offer, and when I walked into the gym, I saw Murillo Bustamante, Mario Sperry, Allan Goes, Vitor Belfort, Ricardo Arona, and Paulo Filho all going at it on the mats. Instantly I knew I had found the right place. And when these fighters decided to band together to form the Brazilian Top Team, I stepped forward and joined them.

Despite getting the training I needed, I lost to Dan Henderson in the King of Kings semifinals. It was a brutal back-and-forth battle, but when all was said and done, he won a split decision. The loss didn't do anything to make my pay go up, but this was back in the day, when the best fighters in the world were only making twenty or thirty thousand dollars a fight. I stuck with it because I loved fighting. As long as I had enough money to pay the rent and put food on the table, I was content.

That contentedness showed in the ring in 2000. I won all of my fights, including the next King of Kings tournament. At that time, the PRIDE Fighting Championships was beginning to take over in Japan. They already had some big names, such as Wanderlei Silva, but they wanted to add more names to their roster. Arona had just won ADCC, the most prestigious no-gi grappling tournament in the world, and I had triumphed in all my fights over experienced competitors, so they came knocking on our doors. We went back and forth with contract negotiations for about six months, but when we finally settled on all the details, I made the transition. Little did I know that in the near future PRIDE would become the largest MMA organization in the world, drawing one hundred thousand spectators to the Tokyo Dome, with ten million more watching at home on television.

They started me off with a bang. I went up against former UFC competitor and heavy-handed striker Gary Goodridge, and when I submitted him via triangle choke, they pitted me against former UFC heavyweight champion and current PRIDE heavyweight champion Mark Coleman. Fighting for the title right out of the gate seemed a little sudden, but I leapt on the chance. Coleman was a good deal larger than I was and had a lot more experience, but I believed in my jiu-jitsu, and it didn't let me down. At a little over six minutes into the first round, I submitted Coleman with a triangle armbar and earned the PRIDE heavyweight title.

I held on to the belt for two years, finishing the majority of my next six opponents with one submission or another. It wasn't easy. Most of my fights had a recurring theme in that my opponents were a good deal heavier than I was. In some cases it was a fifty-pound weight difference, and in other cases it was close to a hundred-pound weight difference. Fighting Bob Sapp was almost ridiculous. His arms were bigger than my legs, and his fists were the size of Thanksgiving turkeys.

Analyzing the heavyweight division, I realized that this trend would most likely continue. I knew that having such large men hovering in your guard throwing ruthless ground and pound could be disastrous, so I spent a lot of time developing various guard control positions that would allow me to hinder my opponent's ability to strike yet still allow me to remain on the offensive. I also worked tirelessly on stringing my attacks together. If my opponent countered one submission, I'd use his defense to immediately transition into another. As you will soon see, this system is what I offer in this book.

I believed in my jiu-jitsu and technique, and as a result I had a great deal of success. Prior to each fight, I analyzed my opponent and then tailored my training to capitalize on his weakness and exploit my strengths. The process worked well for two years, allowing me to retain the title. So when I got matched up with Fedor Emelianenko, I broke him down the best I could. Although I had seen him compete in RINGS, he was still an up-and-coming fighter. I had fought six other Russians from his team, heard them talking good things about his fighting ability, but for the most part my entire camp was hanging in the dark about what to expect. All we knew for sure was that he was in shape and had hard strikes. That didn't seem too daunting—I had fought plenty of guys who were in shape and hit hard. We figured it would be a battle, but nothing I hadn't been in before. No one in my training camp expected him to be as good as he was.

I trained hard for the fight, but I had received a severe spinal injury when I fought Coleman, and it was acting up. Mostly it affected my conditioning, and the last thing you want is to be out of shape when fighting a guy who is in excellent shape. But those were the cards that I was dealt, so I made do.

In March 2003, we squared off in the Yokohama Arena in Japan in front of eighty thousand fans. Knowing that it probably wasn't in my best interest to stand and trade punches, I constantly worked on getting him into my guard. Once there, I went for submissions, sweeps, and transitions, but he did an exceptional job of controlling my wrists and body. He landed a lot of very hard punches, and I kept working my guard game. The nice part about my system is that when your opponent strikes, it allows you to establish one of a number of posture control positions and then begin your attack. But Fedor was smart. To prevent me from establishing these positions, he would drag me toward the edge of the ring and position my head underneath the rope, which prevented me from sitting up into him. Other times, he limited my movement by dragging me into a corner and pressing my head up against the foam backstop. The instant he rendered me immobile, he'd unleash with strikes. And let me tell you, he hits hard. Although I'm not sure when, at one point in the fight he landed a shot that badly injured my jaw.

I fought to the very end. As I have already said, in order to be a good fighter you must believe in your skills and always keep trying. It doesn't matter how badly you are getting beaten. If your opponent knocks you down, you have to get back up. As long as your lights are still on, you're still in the game. I truly believe that, but unfortunately Fedor had my number and was the better fighter that day. As a result, he won the unanimous decision and took the belt. I've had some tough battles over my career, but I'd have to say that that was the toughest. He took me by complete surprise with his agility and fighting ability.

I didn't get much of a break between tough competitors. Later that same year, I took on Mirko "Cro Cop" Filipović, a K-1 fighter who had made the transition over to MMA. At the time, he had destroyed everyone he stepped into the ring with, and in dramatic fashion. They wanted Filipović to fight for the title, but for reasons unknown to me, Fedor had turned down the fight twice. As a result, they matched us up. Although Fedor got to keep his title, they would give a second heavyweight title to the winner of our bout.

When analyzing Filipović's style, I realized that it would be a very interesting matchup. It was striker versus grappler, but he wasn't your classic striker. He had kicks that could literally take your head off, as he had already proven in several of his fights.

I took a lot of punishment from his kicks in the first round, but at the beginning of the second I executed a very good double-leg takedown and brought him down into my world. As I controlled him, he turned a little bit onto his side in an attempt to escape. It was the only opening I needed, and I caught him in an armlock and forced him tap.

A year after my victory over Filipović, I still had a heavyweight belt and Fedor still had a heavyweight belt. In an attempt to resolve this matter, PRIDE held a heavyweight tournament. If all went well during my first fight of the night, I would have to fight the winner on the opposite side of the bracket, which I expected would most likely be Fedor. I had been beaten pretty badly in our first encounter, so I thought to myself, I have to do something different this time around. I called up Dorea, my longtime boxing coach, and asked him his opinion.

"Come down here," he said, referring to Cuba. "I am going to round up some guys for you to train with and give you a camp."

I followed his instructions, and it was brutal. The day started off at 5 AM with a twelve-kilometer run. Next, it was off to hours of grueling fight training. With each passing day, I felt my body growing sharper and stronger, but there were some downsides to the Cuban camp. First off, they only ate two times a day, and they had no meat. In order to get the protein I needed, I had to down dozens of protein shakes and bars. There also was no hot water. After putting your body through unspeakable torture for long hours, it's nice to pamper it with a hot shower and some decent food, but when I walked away from the camp, I realized the lack of luxuries had only made me stronger.

I felt very confident when I stepped into the ring for my first bout of the tournament. My opponent was Sergei Kharitonov, an undefeated Russian fighter. I had heard that he had been training for the Olympics with the Kazakhstani boxing team when he decided to make the transition to MMA. He was as tough as nails, which I wouldn't have minded if Fedor were also fighting a tough-as-nails competitor on his side of the bracket, but he wasn't. He was pitted against Naoya Ogawa, a fighter who I felt was a lot easier to defeat than Kharitonov.

As I suspected, Fedor defeated Ogawa with an armbar in less than a minute, while I fought a hard battle to the decision. Thankfully, the hard work I had put into my training paid off, and I went into the fight with Fedor with some gas still in my tank. Just as with our first encounter, I played guard. I constantly worked to transition to a more dominant position, and then, two and a half minutes in, it looked as if I would be successful. Utilizing an arm drag, I went to take Fedor's back. I don't know if he was tired or what, but he wasn't fighting his normal game that night. As I went to move behind him, he head-butted me. Instead of causing me damage, it opened a cut on his head that instantly began to pour blood. The referee intervened, and it was decided that he couldn't continue.

The problem I had with the fight was that they ruled it a "no contest." Fedor knew that I was going to take his back, and he threw a head butt to stop me. Since the cut wasn't my fault, I felt they should rule the fight in my favor. But as I have learned, sometimes things don't go your way in the fight game. There is no sense making a stink about something you can't control. I agreed to a rematch on New Year's Eve that same year, but just as with the first time we fought, Fedor had my number and rightfully earned a unanimous decision.

After I had six more fights in PRIDE, they closed their doors in 2007, due to financial troubles. With the organization dissolved, I needed to find a new fighting home, and thankfully, the UFC invited me to be a part of their team. I'm not going to lie—it was a tough transition on several levels. For my entire career I had fought in a ring, not a cage. I was accustomed to using my boxing skills to back my opponent into the corner of the ring, which hindered his retreat and allowed me to execute takedowns. In the Octagon, there were no real corners. I also had a disadvantage when it came to throwing elbow strikes on the ground, which was illegal in Japan. I wasn't as concerned about eating elbows while on the bottom because the guard system I had developed worked wonders for stifling my opponent's strikes, but I had to take a crash course on throwing elbows at my opponents when in the top position. Then there was the Vaseline—in Japan, fighters aren't allowed to use it, but in America they smear it on the fighters' faces. It only takes a few good punches to get it all over your hands, and then for the rest of the fight trying to old on to your opponent's arms is like trying to hold a slimly fish. The last thing I had to get used to were the crowds. Although in PRIDE you routinely had a hundred thousand people filling the auditorium, it was so quiet you could hear a pin drop. In the UFC, the fans let their enthusiasm be heard, and it was easy to let all that noise disrupt your concentration.

I was worried about how all these things would affect me, but after I defeated Heath Herring and shook off the rust, I felt just as comfortable in the Octagon as I had in the ring. This was a very good thing, because for my second fight they gave me a shot at Tim Sylvia and the UFC Heavyweight Title. With Sylvia standing almost six feet eight inches tall, I had some trouble dealing with his reach. He rocked my bell several times, but following the mantra of never giving up, I hung in there. When I finally managed to get the fight to the ground and pull guard in the third round, I turned the tied of battle and caught him with a guillotine choke.

It was a big victory for me because it solidified my position in the UFC, the most respected MMA organization in the world. Instead of traveling back and forth to Japan, I can now spend more time in Miami, teaching at my gym and hanging out with my family. Despite having a decent amount of success in the sport, I have never forgotten what truly matters. If not for my family's support and belief in me, I never would be where I am at today. I would probably be working an average job, training in my free time. I owe them everything.

THE MMA GUARD

The guard is what separates Brazilian Jiu-Jitsu from other grappling arts such as judo, sambo, and submission wrestling. For decades, fighters in Brazil have devoted their lives to mastering the position, but it wasn't until Royce Gracie submitted countless fighters off his back in the early days of the UFC that the martial arts world became aware of the position's effectiveness. With fighters from the traditional martial arts having no understanding of how to defend against the guard player's attacks, Brazilian Jiu-Jitsu practitioners reigned supreme in mixed martial arts competition.

As time passed, more and more fighters began training in submission. Wrestlers learned how to nullify the guard player's sweeps and submissions by controlling his hips. They also learned how to use the top position to throw devastating punches. The art of ground and pound was born, casting the guard back into the shadows. To this day, most MMA fighters and fans view the guard as an inferior position. If you're on the bottom, the majority of the time you're considered to be losing the fight.

I don't share this opinion. As long as you're armed with an intricate system, proper technique, and timing, the guard is an extremely dominant position. When I actively competed in Brazilian Jiu-Jitsu back in the day, I always

pulled guard. It just made sense. Fighting off my back allowed me to use both of my arms and both of my legs to attack, while my opponent on top was restricted to using just his arms. Four limbs against two—how could you not like those odds?

Despite the general consensus that guard players were outdated, I had no intention of abandoning the position when I made the transition to MMA. I wasn't ignorant enough to think that I could play the guard exactly the same in a sport where striking was allowed. I knew that in order to be successful fighting off my back, I needed to develop a guard system that would nullify my opponent's ground and pound, yet still allow me to be offensive.

Although it didn't happen overnight, that system eventually materialized through hundreds of hours of training and numerous fights. Today, I use a guard system that allows me to flow seamlessly from one attack to another, all the while protecting myself from my opponent's punches. This is what I share with you in this book.

The system includes control positions from the closed guard, open guard, inside hooks guard, half guard, and downed guard. While it is important to learn how to secure these control positions and then use them to execute offensive techniques, it is just as important to learn how to transition from one control position to the next and string your attacks together. If your opponent counters one control position, he creates an opening to transition to another. If he counters a sweep or submission, the chances are you can use his counter to set-up another attack. It doesn't matter if he blocks ten of your attacks in a row—as long as you constantly base your next attack on your opponent's reactions to your movement, eventually you'll get one step ahead of him.

No matter what type of guard you play, the strategy is always the same—always move and always attack. Lying flat on your back and hanging on for dear life allows your opponent to get offensive and implement his game. It is important to remember that the best defense is always a strong offense.

To help you with the chore of learning how to string your techniques together based upon your opponent's reactions to your movement, I've organized techniques throughout the book into sequences. If you pick and choose which technique to learn, you won't get all that you can out of this manual. It is important to realize that nothing works all of the time, and

seldom does something work the first time. For example, I demonstrate how to lock in a kimura from the sitting-up guard posture control position. It's great when you can finish your opponent with the submission, but the majority of the time he will defend against it by pulling his arm tight to his body. Instead of giving up, I show you how to use his reaction to your advantage by transitioning into a guillotine choke. It's super when you can lock in the guillotine choke, but chances are your opponent will defend against it by pulling your arm away from his neck. Following the golden rule of constantly attacking, I demonstrate how to use his defense to transition directly into a triangle choke. And if he counters the triangle, I again show several ways to capitalize on his defense.

I offer numerous controls, submissions, transitions, and sweeps in this book, as well as demonstrate how to flow between them, but as a guard player, it is your job to add to the system and master your own flow of attacks. The combinations that you can put together are endless, and the deeper you go into that rabbit hole, the more success you will have from the guard.

GUARD KEY CONCEPTS

✳ **Keep your head elevated off the mat.**

✳ **Never stall when playing guard.**

✳ **Stay on the offense by always moving and attacking. Never give up your attack.**

✳ **String your attacks together based on your opponent's reaction to your initial movement.**

✳ **Always look to establish one of the control positions.**

⛏**Always control your opponent's head and posture.**

⛏**Position your head close to your opponent's head to avoid taking damage from strikes.**

⛏**Always work to secure inside control on your opponent's arms.**

✳ **To hinder your opponent from posturing, keep his weight on his knees rather than his ankles.**

In this section I cover all the posture controls that I use from the full guard. They're called "posture controls" because they allow you to do just that—control your opponent's posture. In each position this is achieved by securing your opponent's head and eliminating all space between your bodies. With your opponent's face pinned to your chest or shoulder, his ability to throw straight punches gets eliminated. At that point, his only viable striking option is to throw looping punches. To eliminate that ability as well, you position one or both of your arms to the inside of his arms. Once accomplished, your opponent's offense is heavily stifled, allowing you to begin plotting your attack based upon his reaction to the position.

To get the most out of this section, it is important not to view one posture control as being better than another—they all lead to numerous attacks. Deciding which control to utilize should be based upon your opponent's actions, your strengths, and your goals in the fight. If you're not having luck with one control position, I demonstrate a number of ways to transition into another. No matter which position you assume, your goals are the same: get to your feet, secure a submission, or transition to a dominant position. You will learn multiple ways to accomplish each goal from all the various positions, but in addition to learning the how, you must also learn the when and why. With all of the techniques I show in this section, timing and sensitivity to your opponent's movements are essential.

Unlike most books, I haven't offered a random group of techniques. I've sequenced the moves together based on an opponent's most common reaction to your position or previous submission. If your goal is to develop a guard system where everything is interconnected, I suggest studying this section sequentially.

CLOSED GUARD POSTURE CONTROL

In this portion of the section, you will learn how to establish closed guard posture control, as well as how to execute a number of highly effective submissions based upon your opponent's reaction to the position. The best time to employ this form of control is when your opponent is comfortable lying down in your guard with his head buried in your chest. If he attempts to posture up, you can use your control to break him back down, but you don't want to burn unnecessary energy forcing the position. When he is determined to elevate his head and gets his weight back on his heels, your best option is to sit up with him and transition into either sitting-up posture control or open guard posture control, both of which are covered thoroughly later in the section.

SITTING-UP GUARD POSTURE CONTROL

If you're having trouble breaking your opponent down into your guard or he is broken down in your guard and determined to posture up, the sitting-up posture control guard is an excellent position to assume. In this part of the section I demonstrate several methods for securing the position, as well as how to use the position to execute a series of submissions, starting with the kimura. Again, the majority of techniques are based upon your opponent's counter to your previous attack, making it important to start this part of the section at the beginning. If you take the time to master each technique and the way it's set up, you'll be able to flow from one to the next until you get one step ahead of your opponent and secure a submission.

OPEN GUARD POSTURE CONTROL

Like the sitting-up posture control guard, the open guard posture control position is best utilized when you are unable to break your opponent down due to his strong posture. Once you obtain the position, you have two routes you can take. The first is to create space between you and your opponent, which allows you to make a quick escape back to your feet. The second route is to transition to the omaplata position, which in turn leads to a series of sequenced attacks. As you would expect, the first attack in the sequence is the omaplata shoulder-lock submission, but if your opponent defends against it, you can use his defense to execute a number of highly effective sweeps and transitions, all of which are covered in this portion of the section.

Technical Note: Throughout this section you'll notice that I demonstrate the posture control positions and attacks on just one side of my opponent's body. For example, in each technique I obtain control of my opponent's head with my left hand and secure inside biceps control with my right hand. It's beneficial to focus on mastering one side in the beginning, but your goal is to become a dangerous guard player, you must eventually master both sides. After all, if your opponent realizes that you can only attack his right arm with an omaplata, he doesn't have to worry about defending his left arm, making it much harder for you to lock in the submission. However, if you have the ability to randomly switch sides with your control positions and attacks, you force your opponent to spread his focus thin, increasing your chances of catching him off guard.

HEAD AND ARM CONTROL (NEUTRALIZING THE ATTACK)

Before you begin practicing dynamic submissions and elaborate sweeps from the guard, it is important to understand basic positioning. The goal is to assume a position that neutralizes your opponent's attacks, yet still allows you to employ attacks of your own. This can be achieved in two simple steps.

The first step is to control your opponent's posture so you can dictate distance and close off all space between your bodies, making it nearly impossible for him to throw straight strikes at your centerline. With his posture broken, his only real striking option is to target the sides of your body with looping punches, which leads us to the second step in basic positioning—securing inside control on your opponent's arms. Positioning your arms to the inside of your opponent's arms solidifies your defense. Every time your opponent throws a looping punch toward the side of your head, you can catch his biceps with your hand or elbow to prevent his fist from reaching your face.

To achieve both steps in a fight, I frequently utilize head and arm control. If you look at the photos in the sequence below, you'll notice that I have my left hand hooked around the back of my opponent's head and that I use that control to pin his forehead to my chest. With all space between our bodies closed off, his ability to throw straight punches is eliminated. To protect the right side of my face from his looping punches, I have cupped my right hand over his left biceps. If he were to throw a left-handed strike, I could immediately stop it by applying outward pressure using my right hand. With my left hand busy keeping my opponent's posture broken, the left side of my face is slightly more vulnerable, so I protect my face by hiding my head to the right of my opponent's head. If my opponent were to throw a looping right-handed strike, I could also angle my left elbow outward to block his arm at the biceps and check his punch.

Once you achieve head and arm control, the goal is to force a reaction out of your opponent, and then use that reaction to transition into a submission, a dominant position, or an escape back to your feet. Each of the control positions covered in the upcoming sections can be attained from head and arm control, including sitting-up guard posture control, closed guard posture control, and open guard posture control. For example, if your opponent fights your head control and postures up, you can sit up with him, establish sitting-up guard posture control or open guard posture control, and then work your attacks. If he remains broken down in your head and arm control, then you can transition into closed guard posture control, which is the next technique presented in this section. The one thing you don't want to do from head and arm control is stall. It is important to always move and attack. When you remain on the offensive, your opponent has to constantly counter your movement, which means he is defending rather than attacking.

I have Feijao in my closed guard. To control his posture, I cup my left hand around the back of his head and then use that control to pin his face to my chest. To protect myself from his looping left punches, I cup my right hand over his left biceps, and to protect myself from his looping right punches, I hide my head to the right of his head. As you can see, it is very difficult for my opponent to land effective strikes from this position.

Feijao pulls his right arm back to throw a looping punch to my face.

Keeping Feijao's head pinned to my chest using my left hand, I roll slightly onto my right shoulder and angle my left elbow outward, catching his right biceps with my left forearm. With my head still elevated off the mat and positioned to the right of Feijao's head, I prevent his fist from reaching the side of my face and take zero damage.

Having failed to land his overhand right, Feijao draws his left arm back to throw a looping punch to the right side of my face. To maintain my defensive posture, I keep his head pinned to my chest and my right hand positioned to the inside of his left arm.

As Feijao's punch approaches, I flare my right elbow out slightly and catch his left biceps with my right forearm, stopping his punch before his fist can reach my face.

BREAKING OPPONENT DOWN TO CLOSED GUARD POSTURE CONTROL

A lot of times when you have an opponent in your guard, he will place his hands on your hips and posture up to strike or pass your guard. Instead of letting him remain in this position and be offensive, you want to break his posture down and obtain control of his body and movements. In this sequence, I demonstrate how to accomplish this by establishing closed guard posture control. While securing head and arm control is a great way to quickly neutralize your opponent's attack, you should always be looking to secure closed guard posture control or one of the other control positions I cover later in the book. Not only do they make it easier to keep your opponent broken down, but they also lead to numerous attacks.

Technical Note: There are countless grips that you can employ from closed guard posture control, but through training and fighting, I've found the ten-finger grip demonstrated below to not only be the strongest grip, but also the best suited for this specific position.

Feijao is in my closed guard. His hands are on my hips and he is postured up. To limit his offensive options and increase mine, I decide to break him down into closed guard posture control.

To clear Feijao's control and break his posture, I drive my left hand to the inside of his right arm and then curl my legs inward. The combination of these actions forces his left hand off of my hips and he falls forward into my guard. If I had neglected to drive my left hand underneath Feijao's right arm before pulling my knees toward my chest, he could have used his left hand on my hip as a brace and prevented me from collapsing him forward.

As Feijao falls forward, I slip my left arm underneath his right arm and reach my right arm around the back of his head. It is important to note that once you collapse your opponent forward, you must secure control of his body quickly to prevent him from posturing back up.

Having slipped my left arm underneath Feijao's right arm, I reach my left hand toward my right. At the same time, I position my right forearm in front of his left shoulder.

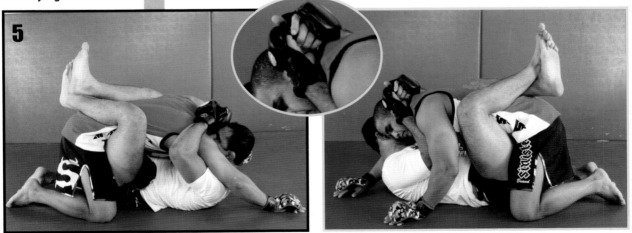

To secure closed guard posture control, I wrap my left arm around the back of Feijao's right shoulder and then clasp my hands together behind his neck using a ten-finger grip. Since I established the underhook with my left arm, my left palm is facing down and my right palm is facing up. This positioning allows me to pull the right side of his body toward me using my left arm, and push the left side of his body away from me by driving my right forearm into his shoulder. With his right side pinned to me, it becomes very difficult for him to strike with his right hand. And with my right elbow controlling his left side, it is very difficult for him to strike with his left hand. To further protect myself, I keep my head elevated off the mat and my face buried in Feijao's right shoulder. It is also important to note that I am still curling my legs into my body, which keeps Feijao on his knees rather than his heels and makes it much more difficult for him to posture up. From here, I will keep my control loose enough to execute an attack, but tight enough to prevent Feijao from escaping the position.

SEQUENCE A: BLOCKING PUNCHES FROM CLOSED GUARD POSTURE CONTROL

I've secured the closed guard posture control position on Feijao.

With his right arm completely trapped, Feijao attempts to throw a looping punch at my head using his left arm. To prevent his fist from reaching the side of my face, I flare my right elbow slightly out to the side, catching his left biceps. Although blocking this strike is quite easy, it is very important to keep your ten-finger grip tight. You also want to maintain downward pressure with your left arm and outward pressure with your right forearm.

As Feijao pulls his left arm back, I angle my right elbow inward and continue to apply outward pressure to his shoulder. From here, I will immediately begin my attack.

BLOCK OVERHAND TO CLOSED GUARD POSTURE CONTROL

In this sequence I demonstrate how to establish the closed guard posture control position while countering your opponent's ground and pound. Below, my opponent postures up in my guard, but before I can use the previous technique to break him down, he pulls his right hand back to throw an overhand punch. Immediately I draw my legs toward my torso to pull him forward. As he falls into my guard, I elevate my left arm to block his punch. Then, in one fluid motion, I swim my left arm underneath his right arm, position my right forearm in front of his left shoulder, and establish the closed guard posture control position by securing a ten-finger grip behind his head. As you might imagine, timing is very important when executing this technique. The instant your opponent pulls his arm back to punch, use your legs to pull him down into your guard. When your timing is right, it will strip the majority of power from his punch and make it easy to obtain control of his body. If your timing is off, your chances of adequately blocking the strike and securing control drop dramatically.

Feijao is postured up in my closed guard with his hands on my hips.

Before I can break Feijao's posture and establish control of his body, he cocks his right hand back to throw a looping punch at my head.

POSTURE CONTROL

As Feijao's fist nears my face, I sit up, roll slightly onto my right hip, move my head toward my right side, and elevate my left arm.

As I catch Feijao's right arm with the outside of my left forearm, I angle my left hand toward the back of my head. This causes his right arm to slide down my left forearm and toward the mat behind me. At the same time, I curl my knees toward my chest, breaking his balance and forcing him to lurch forward into my guard.

Having prevented Feijao's right fist from colliding with my face, I quickly punch my left arm underneath his right arm and allow his momentum to carry him forward into my guard. At the same time, I move my right forearm in front of his left shoulder.

As Feijao falls forward, I swim my left arm underneath his right arm and secure a ten-finger grip behind his neck. Because I established an underhook with my left arm, my left palm is facing down and my right palm is facing up. With my grip intact, I drive my right forearm into his left shoulder and pull his right shoulder into me using my left arm. To further protect myself, I keep my head elevated off the mat and position my face between Feijao's right arm and head. From this position, I have several options to attack.

ARM TRIANGLE

All the attacks from the closed guard posture control position begin the same. If you have your opponent's head and right arm trapped as I do in the sequence below, you begin by posting your left foot on the mat and shrimping your hips out from underneath his body. At the same time, you shrug your left shoulder into his right arm to escape your head out from underneath his trapped arm. Executing both actions in one explosive movement allows you to reposition your body off to your opponent's side, opening up numerous attack options. In the sequence below, I demonstrate how to apply the arm triangle submission from this position. Although it's a low-risk submission that is relatively simple due to few steps being involved, it can be a difficult submission to finish. To force your opponent to submit, you need to position the inside of you right wrist against the left side of his neck. In addition to this, you need to drive his right shoulder into the right side of his neck. Unless you accomplish both, you will not cut off blood flow to your opponent's brain.

I've secured the closed guard posture control position on Feijao.

To begin my attack, I open my guard and post my left foot on the mat.

In one explosive movement, I push off the mat with my left foot, shrug my left shoulder into Feijao's right arm, and escape my hips toward my left side.

Maintaining a tight ten-finger grip, I escape my head out from underneath Feijao's right arm and roll onto my right shoulder and hip. Due to my positioning, I am able to trap his right arm to my chest and wrap the crook of my right arm underneath his chin. If I had failed to come up onto my right hip and shoulder, it would have been very difficult to trap my opponent's right arm, allowing him to posture up, break my control, and escape.

Keeping Feijao's right arm pinned to my chest and my right arm curled tight around his neck, I straighten my left arm and prepare to establish a figure-four lock.

I grab my left biceps with my right hand, curl my left arm back, and then grip the top of Feijao's head with my left hand. To finish the arm triangle submission, I squeeze my arms together using all my strength. Notice how my right forearm is digging into the left side of his neck, and I'm forcing his right shoulder into the right side of his neck. With blood flow to his brain severed, he has no choice but to tap.

TRANSITIONING TO BACK CONTROL

Transitioning to your opponent's back is another excellent option when you secure the closed guard posture control position. The technique is set up in the same manner as the arm triangle—escape your hips out from under your opponent's body and clear your head out from underneath his trapped arm. However, instead of applying a figure-four lock on his head, you circle around to his back, establish control of his body, and begin your attack. If you're up against an opponent who is a master at escaping the arm triangle or you'd rather work for a submission from a more dominant position, this is a very good technique to have in your arsenal.

I've secured the closed guard posture control position on Feijao.

To begin my attack, I open my guard and post my left foot on the mat.

In one explosive movement, I push off the mat with my left foot, shrug my left shoulder into Feijao's right arm, and escape my hips toward my left side. Notice how I turn onto my right side, escaping my entire body out from underneath my opponent.

As I escape my head out from underneath Feijao's right arm, I scoot my hips further toward my left side, position my head over his right arm, and squeeze my grip tight. The combination of these actions traps his right arm between my right arm and head, making it difficult for him to posture up as I prepare for my transition to his back.

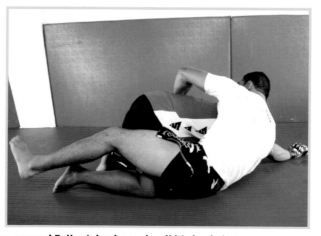

In one fluid motion, I release my grip, sit up, hook my left arm around Feijao's body, and pull his body into me.

Continuing to pull Feijao's body into mine using my left arm, I step my left foot over his right leg and post my right hand on the mat.

Still pulling on Feijao's hip with my left arm, I push off the mat using my right hand and left foot, pull myself onto his back, and hook my right leg around the inside of his right leg.

To secure control of Feijao's back, I need to hook my left foot around the inside of his left leg, but he prevents me from accomplishing this by pinning his left elbow to his left knee, closing off all space. In order to open a gap to slide my foot in, I jam my left hand underneath his left armpit and grab his left wrist with my left hand.

9

Using my left grip, I pull Feijao's left arm underneath his body and drive my left forearm into the back of his shoulder.

10

I drive my right leg into Feijao's right leg and I push my body forward. Notice how this spreads him out and creates a gap between his left elbow and left thigh. Immediately I throw my left leg over his back and dig my foot into that gap.

11

I slide my left leg to the inside of Feijao's left leg, establishing my second hook. Next, I drive my hips into his lower back and sprawl my legs back. The combination of my actions flattens him belly down to the mat and eliminates much of his defense. From here, I will begin striking the sides of his head with punches or begin working for a choke.

STRAIGHT ARMBAR

As you now know, escaping your hips and head out from underneath your opponent allows you to lock in an arm triangle or transition to his back when in closed guard posture control. Both techniques are highly effective, but neither is foolproof. If your opponent is an experienced grappler, his first reaction to either technique will be to posture up and pull his trapped arm free. A strong grip and quick movements are often enough to prevent his escape, but if he manages to get the upper hand and achieve his goals, you can use his defensive movements against him by transitioning to the armbar I demonstrate in the sequence below. In this day and age, the majority of martial artists competing in MMA have very sharp submission defense. If your goal is to win fights by submission, you must have the ability to string techniques together based on your opponent's reactions.

I've secured the closed guard posture control position on Feijao.

I post my left foot on the mat and begin to escape my hips toward my left side.

3

Pushing off the mat with my left foot, I elevate my hips into Feijao's right side, shrug my left shoulder into his right arm, and escape my head out from underneath his right arm.

4

As I pull my head out from underneath Feijao's right arm, I scoot my hips further to my left side, position my head over his right arm, and squeeze my grip tight. The combination of these actions traps his right arm between my right arm and head.

5

Before I can lock in an arm triangle or transition to his back, Feijao posts his left hand on the mat and elevates his head.

Instead of resisting Feijao's escape attempt, I use his reaction to my advantage by elevating my hips toward my left side and throwing my left leg over his right shoulder. Notice that I've kept my ten-finger grip intact. If you release your grip, your opponent will continue to posture and escape the submission.

I wrap my left leg over the top of Feijao's right shoulder, hook my right foot over my left foot, and apply downward pressure with both legs. Notice how these actions trap his right arm to my chest. Next, I release my ten-finger grip, hook my right arm over his trapped right arm, and reach my left hand toward my right side.

Now that I have Feijao's body under control, I need to move his weight off of me. To begin this process, I grab the back of his left elbow with my left hand.

With my right arm still hooked over the top of Feijao's right arm, I pull his left elbow toward the left side of my body using my left grip on his triceps. Not only does this action cross his left arm over his right arm, but it also moves his weight in the direction of my legs, taking pressure off of my hips.

With much of Feijao's weight off of my upper body, I throw my left leg over his head and circle my hips in a counterclockwise direction. Notice that I'm still using my right arm to keep his right arm pinned to my chest.

I wrap my left leg around the left side of Feijao's head. To prevent him from posturing up and escaping the position, I curl my left leg down into his head and my right leg down into the left side of his back.

Still controlling both of Feijao's arms and applying downward pressure with my legs, his balance is disrupted and he falls to his right side.

As I force Feijao to his back, I grab his right arm with both of my hands. It is important to notice my grip. I've wrapped my right thumb around his right thumb and then wrapped the rest of my right fingers around the outside of his thumb and the top of his hand. This grip provides optimal control, and it also allows me to turn his arm so that his right thumb is pointing straight up, which is mandatory for the submission to work. To finish the armbar, I pull his right arm into my chest, curl my legs down into his head and body, pinch my knees together, and elevate my hips into his elbow.

SECURING SITTING-UP POSTURE CONTROL

When you have an opponent in your guard, you never want to try to force a control position. If you're having a difficult time breaking him down into closed guard posture control, transitioning to the sitting-up guard posture control position is an excellent option. It's also a great option when you have your opponent broken down in your guard, and he forces his head up. Instead of burning precious energy battling to keep his head down, you sit up with him and then set up an attack from sitting-up guard posture control. Learning how to transition between the various control positions I offer in this book is mandatory because it allows you to react to your opponent's movements. In the sequence below, I demonstrate how to secure the sitting-up guard posture control position when your opponent is postured up and has his hands on your hips.

Feijao is postured up in my closed guard with his hands on my hips.

I slide my right arm underneath Feijao's left arm.

I clear Feijao's left hand off my hip by circling my right hand toward my right side. Next, I hook my right hand around the inside of his left biceps and secure inside control on his arm.

Keeping my right hand hooked around the inside of Feijao's left arm, I draw my knees toward my chest, sit up, and reach my left hand toward the right side of his head.

Rolling slightly onto my right shoulder, I hook my left hand around the back of Feijao's neck and pull his head down. It is important to notice that I hook my hand around the top of his neck rather than the bottom. With this control, I can force his chin to his chest and break his posture. If I were to form my grip lower, he could elevate his chin and straighten his posture, preventing me from establishing the sitting-up guard posture control position.

Now that I have control of Feijao's head and established inside control on his left arm, I hook my right foot over his left leg. This prevents him from hopping over my right leg, passing my guard, and securing side control.

I kick my left leg toward the mat and use that momentum to sit up. Notice how I keep my head positioned to the right of Feijao's head.

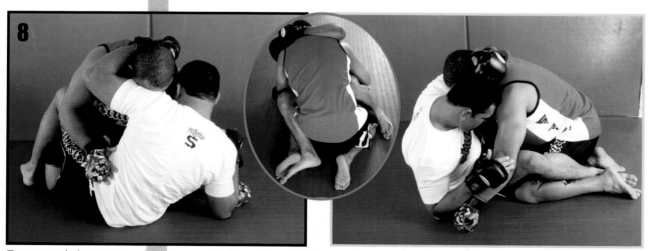

To secure sitting-up guard posture control, I post my left foot on the mat, post on my right elbow, and tuck my head between Feijao's left shoulder and head. It's important to mention that I'm pulling his head into my left shoulder to keep him on his knees, which prevents him from posturing. From here, I will immediately begin my attack.

SEQUENCE A: **PROTECTING YOUR HEAD**

I've secured the sitting-up guard posture control position on Feijao.

With his right arm free, Feijao attempts to punch me in the face.

Since I'm controlling Feijao's posture with my left arm, pulling his head into my left shoulder, and hiding my head behind the left side of his head, his fist lands to the back of my shoulder. Not only does his punch have little power, but it also completely misses its target. However, if I were to loosen up my control, he would be able to create separation and strike my exposed left side.

BLOCK OVERHAND TO SITTING-UP GUARD POSTURE CONTROL

In this sequence, my opponent postures up in my guard and throws a powerful overhand. Although there are many other strikes at his disposal, the overhand is one of the most common due to its power. When faced with such an assault, a lot of opponents will remain flat on their back and attempt to block the strike using their arm. Such a tactic may prevent the strike from hitting their face, but they often absorb a portion of the blow, which can leave them dazed. In addition to this, the tactic does nothing to stop more downward strikes. In my opinion, a much better way to combat this situation is to use the opening created by your opponent's punch to establish the sitting-up guard posture control position. The instant your opponent cocks his hand back to throw the strike, open your guard, move your head offline from the punch, and sit up. If you look at the photos below, you'll notice that I reach my left hand up and grip the back of my opponent's head. This simple action achieves several things—it gives me control of my opponent's posture, prevents his punch from reaching my face, and hinders him from throwing additional punches. Once you secure the sitting-up guard posture control position, you can immediately get your offensive going by attacking your opponent's arm with a kimura, which I demonstrate how to do in the following sequence.

Feijao is postured up in my closed guard with his hands on my hips.

Feijao cocks his right hand back to throw a powerful overhand punch at my face. The instant I see him draw his arm back, I move my head toward my right side, reach my left hand toward the right side of his head, and begin sitting up. Notice how my left arm is now in the path of the punch.

As Feijao follows through with his punch, I open my guard, wrap my left hand around the back of his head, and continue sitting up. Notice how my left arm prevents his punch from reaching my face.

Posting on my right elbow, I pull Feijao's head into my left shoulder, throw my right leg over his left leg, and secure the sitting-up guard posture control position. From here, I can immediately begin my attack.

KIMURA

When you transition to the sitting-up guard posture control position, your opponent will often plant his hands on the mat. His goal is to use his hands to posture up, break your control, and create enough room to strike. However, the instant he plants his hands on the mat, he gives you the space you need to secure a kimura lock on his near arm. Once you have the hold, escape your hips, fall to your side, and then finish the submission. If your opponent is alert to the position and keeps his arms tight to his body to prevent you from locking in the kimura, then you'll want to use his defense to transition into one of the other attacks covered in this section.

I've established the sitting-up guard posture control position on Feijao. In an attempt to posture up and break my control, he plants his left fist on the mat. Immediately I begin setting up the kimura by grabbing his left wrist with my right hand.

Keeping my right hand locked tight around Feijao's left wrist, I reach my left arm over his head and toward the back of his left arm.

To establish a kimura lock, I hook my left arm around Feijao's' upper arm and then grab my right wrist with my left hand.

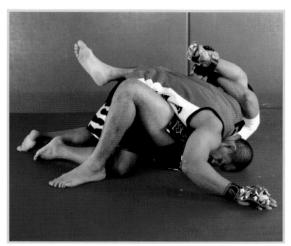

Keeping Feijao's left arm locked tight to my chest, I fall to my right shoulder and scoot my hips toward my right side. To finish the kimura lock, I throw my right leg over Feijao's left hip, roll toward my left shoulder, draw my left arm toward my chest, and push his left wrist over his back using my right hand. It is important to notice the positioning of my body. To make the submission work, you need to slide your body out from underneath your opponent so that you're angled off to the side. If you fail to acquire this angle, your chances of finishing your opponent with the submission drop dramatically.

FAILED KIMURA TO GUILLOTINE

In this sequence, I apply a kimura lock on my opponent's posted left arm, but he blocks the submission by pulling his arm tight to his body. As I have already mentioned, it can often be difficult to submit your opponent with your first attack. Instead of giving up and returning to posture control, I make use of my opponent's reaction and immediately transition into a guillotine choke. If you take a close look at the photos below, you'll notice that my opponent jumps over my posted leg in an attempt to escape the guillotine. When faced with such a scenario, trap your opponent in your half guard. Although it may seem like he just improved his position, he actually allowed you to make the choke tighter. With this submission, the more you can get onto your side, the more leverage you have to finish the guillotine. If your opponent remains in your full guard instead of jumping over your posted leg, you can still finish the submission. Just wrap your legs around your opponent's waist and cinch down with the choke. To learn how this is done, see the next technique in this section.

Technical Note: It is important to mention that I don't just utilize the guillotine off a failed kimura. If at any time my opponent hops over my posted leg when I'm in the sitting-up guard posture control position, I will immediately wrap my arm around the back of his head, cup his chin, and start locking in the guillotine. If he turns back into me to defend, I will either try to finish the submission or let go of the hold, reclaim control of his posture, and plot my next attack.

I've secured the sitting-up guard posture control position on Feijao. With his left fist planted on the mat, I immediately grab his wrist with my right hand to set up the kimura submission.

In an attempt to lock in the kimura, I reach my left arm over Feijao's head and toward my right side.

    MASTERING MIXED MARTIAL ARTS

I attempt to hook my left arm around the back of Feijao's left arm and lock in the kimura, but he defends against my attack by pulling his left arm tight to his body.

The instant Feijao blocks the kimura, I transition to the guillotine choke by wrapping my left arm around the back of his head.

I wrap my left arm tighter around Feijao's head.

I hook my left thumb underneath Feijao's jaw to prevent him from dropping his chin to his chest and blocking the choke. At the same time, I cup my left hand underneath his chin.

Having secured a firm grip on Feijao's chin, I post my right fist on the mat.

Driving off the mat with my right hand, I scoot my hips toward my right side and drop my left shoulder toward the mat. When you make this transition, it is very important to keep a tight grip on your opponent's chin.

9

As I fall to my left side, I throw my right leg over Feijao's back and apply downward pressure. This prevents him from elevating his butt into the air and taking pressure off his neck. At the same time, I hook my right arm around the back of his left arm. Next, I wrap the fingers of my right hand around the outside of my left wrist, forming a solid grip.

10

Feijao steps his right leg over my left leg in an attempt to pass my guard. As he does this, I hook my left leg around the inside of his left leg and trap him in my half guard.

11

By passing into the half guard, Feijao has only made the choke tighter. Remember, the more you can get on your side, the tighter the choke gets. To finish the submission, I pinch my elbows together and pull the inside of my left wrist into Feijao's throat using my right hand. It is important to note that by grabbing your wrist instead clasping your hands together, you not only make it more difficult for your opponent to pull his head free, but you also make the choke tighter.

CLOSED GUARD GUILLOTINE

In the previous guard technique, I attempted to apply a kimura on my opponent, he defended by pulling his arm tight to his body, and I immediately transitioned to a guillotine choke. In an attempt to escape the guillotine choke, my opponent hopped over my posted leg, but I used his defense against him by trapping him in the half guard, which allowed me to lock the choke tighter. In this sequence I make the exact same transition from a failed kimura to the guillotine, but now I demonstrate how to finish the guillotine from the closed guard. Both finishes are equally as effective—deciding which one to apply boils down to how your opponent reacts to the submission. If he hops over your grounded leg, utilize the previous technique. If he remains in your guard or you can wrap your legs around him before he has a chance to hop over your leg, utilize the technique demonstrated below.

I've secured the sitting-up guard posture control position on Feijao. With his left hand posted on the mat, I immediately begin setting up the kimura by grabbing his left wrist with my right hand.

I attempt to hook my left arm around the back of Feijao's left arm to lock in the kimura, but he defends by pulling his left arm tight to his body.

Immediately I transition to the guillotine choke by wrapping my left arm around the back of Feijao's head.

I hook my left thumb underneath Feijao's jaw and cup my hand underneath his chin. These actions prevent him from dropping his chin to his chest and blocking the choke.

Having secured a firm grip on Feijao's chin, I post my right fist on the mat.

Driving off the mat with my right hand, I scoot my hips toward my right side and begin dropping my left shoulder toward the mat.

Maintaining my grip on Feijao's chin, I fall to my left side and hook my left leg around his right side to prevent him from passing my guard.

I throw my right leg over Feijao's back and then hook my right foot over my left foot, trapping Feijao in my closed guard. At the same time, I wrap my right arm around the back of his left arm and grab my left wrist with my right hand. Once I have a solid grip, I finish the submission by pinching my elbows together, pulling the blade of my left wrist into his throat using my right hand, and straightening my legs to force his hips back. It is important to notice that I'm lying on my left side. If you're flat on your back, the chances that you'll finish your opponent with the submission drop dramatically.

FAILED GUILLOTINE TO TRIANGLE

When you apply a guillotine choke on an opponent in your guard, chances are he will attempt to peel your fingers off his chin or break your grip apart. If he manages either, the choke is lost. Instead of burning precious energy trying to hang on to his head, a much better option is to transition into another submission. In this sequence, I demonstrate how to use your opponent's guillotine defense to transition into a triangle choke when you've got him captured in your closed guard. To see alternate finishes for the triangle, visit the double wrist control section of the book.

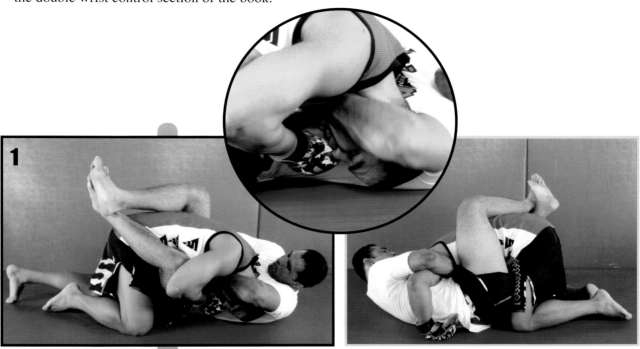

1 I've got Feijao in my closed guard and I'm working to finish him with a guillotine choke. To defend against the submission, he is attempting to break my grip apart using his right hand.

2 Instead of burning energy trying to finish the guillotine, I decide to use Feijao's defense to transition into a triangle choke. To begin, I release his neck and immediately grab his right wrist with my left hand.

I pull my right arm out from underneath Feijao's body, open my guard, and push Feijao's right arm toward his hips using my left hand. Notice how my actions create a pathway for me to throw my left leg over his right shoulder.

I hook my left leg over Feijao's right shoulder and the back of his neck.

I hook my left foot underneath my right leg, trapping Feijao's left arm and head between my legs.

In order to finish the triangle choke, I need to position Feijao's left arm across his neck. To accomplish this, I grab his left arm with both of my hands, elevate my hips, and force his arm toward the left side of my body.

Using my left hand, I pin Feijao's left arm to my left leg. Next, I release my right grip on his arm, drop my hips to the mat, grab my left shin with my right hand, and pull my left leg toward my head. This last action forces my left calf across the back of Feijao's head and allows me to hook my left foot under the crook of my right leg.

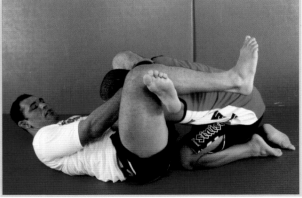

Keeping Feijao's left arm pinned to my left leg, I finish the triangle choke my curling my right leg down into my left leg and squeezing everything tight. If your opponent doesn't tap immediately when you reach this position, you can lock the choke tighter by pulling his head toward your abdomen using both hands.

FAILED KIMURA TO MOUNT TRANSITION

As you now know, the kimura is an excellent submission to apply when you reach the sitting-up guard posture control position and your opponent places his hand on the mat. If he defends against the kimura by pulling his arm tight to his body, you can immediately transition to the guillotine choke as previously shown or you can use the technique demonstrated below to transition to the mount. The latter is an excellent option when you're up against an opponent who has strong submission defense from the guard. Instead of trying to submit him from a position where you have little leverage, you flip him over to his back and obtain a position where you have a ton of leverage. The key to success with this technique is timing—you must execute all the steps in one fluid movement. When done properly, the sweep will seem effortless.

I've secured the sitting-up guard posture control position on Feijao. With his left fist planted on the mat, I immediately begin setting up the kimura by grabbing his left wrist with my right hand.

I attempt to hook my left arm around the back Feijao's left arm to lock in a kimura, but he defends by pulling his left arm tight to his body. I decide to use his defense to transition to the mount.

The instant Feijao blocks the kimura, I jam my left fist to the inside of his left thigh.

I straighten my left arm and wedge my left fist deeper between his legs. It is important to note that the back of my left fist is flush with the inside of his left leg.

I post my right fist on the mat.

Pushing off the mat with my right hand, I scoot my hips toward my right side, straighten my left arm, and drive my left elbow down into the back of Feijao's left arm. With his left arm trapped between my arm and hips, the downward pressure forces his head to the mat.

To acquire the angle I need to finish the submission, I scoot my hips toward my right, drive my left elbow into the back of Feijao's left arm, and rotate my body in a counterclockwise direction.

Having broken Feijao's posture, I rip my left arm out from underneath his body. Next, I post my left hand on the mat behind me and reach my right arm over his back.

I hook my right hand around Feijao's right hip and then pull his body close to mine. Next, I elevate my hips into his hips and force his legs together by drawing my left leg toward my body. This last step is very important. If you allow your opponent to keep his legs spread apart, he will be able to brace himself and block the sweep. Forcing them together eliminates his balance, making it easy to force him over to his back.

Having been fluid with my movements, Feijao gets swept over to his back.

As I roll Feijao to his back, I follow him over and land in the mount. To secure the position, I hook my feet underneath his legs and drive my hips forward. If you fail to immediately stabilize the position, your opponent can use the momentum of the sweep to his advantage by bridging over his shoulder and rolling you to your back.

FAILED KIMURA TO BACK TRANSITION

In this sequence I demonstrate how to transition to your opponent's back when he defends against the kimura from the sitting-up guard posture control position. It is set up the same way as the mount transition in that you jam your hand to the inside of your opponent's leg and escape your hips to break his posture, but instead of elevating your hips into his hips and executing a sweep, you throw your leg over his back, hook your feet to the inside of his legs, and transition to his back. Personally, I feel the mount transition is safer because it requires fewer steps. In one explosive movement, you flip your opponent over to his back and establish a very dominant position. However, that doesn't mean the technique shown in this sequence isn't an excellent transition. If your opponent is tired and you feel you have a good chance of locking in a choke from the back, the technique shown below could be your best option. The important part is making your decision quickly and then committing to it. When your opponent defends against the kimura, you only have a split second to capitalize.

Technical Note: When you escape your hips out from underneath your opponent to take his back, he will sometimes try to turn into you, grab your posted arm, and drive your back to the mat. In such a scenario, transitioning to the mount using the previous technique is a much better option than trying to take his back.

I've secured Feijao in the sitting-up guard posture control position. With his left hand posted on the mat, I immediately begin transitioning to the kimura.

In an attempt to lock in the kimura, I reach my left hand to the left side of Feijao's head.

I try to hook my left arm around the back of Feijao's left arm to lock in the kimura, but he defends by pulling his arm tight to his body.

The instant Feijao blocks the kimura, I wedge my left fist between his legs. It is important to note that the back of my fist is flush with the inside of his left leg.

I post my right fist on the mat.

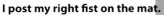

Pushing off the mat with my right hand, I scoot my hips toward my right side. Next, I straighten my left arm and drive my elbow down into the back of Feijao's left arm. With his arm trapped between my arm and hips, the downward pressure forces his head toward the mat.

To acquire the angle I need to make the transition to Feijao's back, I continue to scoot my hips toward my right side. To prevent him from posturing up, I continue to drive my left elbow downward into his left arm.

I post my left elbow on the mat, reach my right hand over Feijao's back, grip his right hip using my right hand, and pull his hips into my body. At the same time, I elevate my hips and pull my left leg out from underneath his body.

I hook my left leg around the inside of Feijao left leg and start climbing onto his back. Notice how I flare my left knee out toward my left side. This forces his left leg to straighten, which spreads out his base, flattens his body to the mat, and prevents him from climbing to his knees and defending my transition.

In order to secure control of Feijao's back, I need to establish an over-under body lock. To begin this process, I jam my left fist between the left side of his neck and shoulder.

I secure an over-under body lock by wrapping my left arm around the left side of Feijao's neck, hooking my right arm underneath his right armpit, and clasping my hands together in the center of his chest.

With my over-under body lock secure, I work on establishing my second hook by throwing my right leg over the top of Feijao's back. It is important to notice that I'm using my over-under body lock and my left hook to keep him spread out and broken down. It is also important to notice that my right underhook is preventing him from dropping his right elbow to his right knee and closing off the gap I need to establish my second hook.

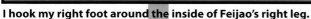

I hook my right foot around the inside of Feijao's right leg.

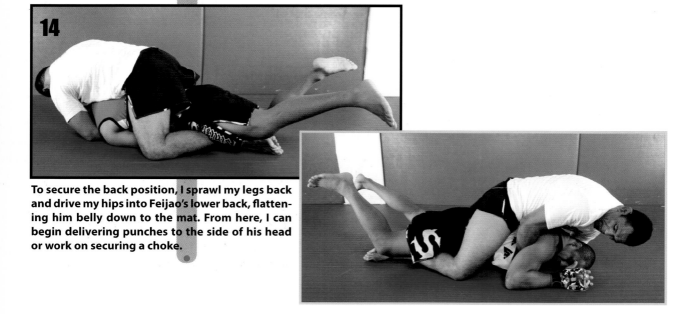

To secure the back position, I sprawl my legs back and drive my hips into Feijao's lower back, flattening him belly down to the mat. From here, I can begin delivering punches to the side of his head or work on securing a choke.

SECURING OPEN GUARD POSTURE CONTROL

In this sequence I demonstrate how to establish the open guard posture control position when an opponent places his hands on your hips and postures up in your guard. In addition to making it very difficult for your opponent to strike, it also creates an opportunity to escape back to your feet or transition into the omaplata position, which leads to the omaplata submission and several other attacks.

Feijao has placed his hands on my hips and postured up in my guard. In order to break his posture, I need to clear his hands off my hips. To begin this process, I dig my right hand underneath his left arm.

I slide my right arm underneath Feijao's left arm and then begin circling my arm toward my right side. Notice how this action pulls his left hand off of my hip.

I hook my right hand around the inside of his Feijao's left biceps to secure inside control on his arm. At the same time, I reach my left hand toward the back of his head and draw my knees toward my chest to pull his upper body forward.

Opening my guard, I place my left foot on the mat, wrap my left hand around the base of Feijao's skull, and pull his head down.

Continuing to pull Feijao's head down and control the inside of his left arm, I push off the mat with my left foot and escape my hips toward my left side.

As I shrimp my hips toward my left side, I draw my right knee toward my body and slip it to the inside of Feijao's left arm.

I place my right foot on Feijao's left hip and position my right knee in front of his left shoulder.

Continuing to pull Feijao's head down with my left hand, I place my left foot on his right hip and pinch my knees together. To secure open guard posture control, I grab his left triceps with my right hand and pin his arm to my right shin. With this position, I make it very difficult for my opponent to posture up or strike.

GROUND AND POUND DEFENSE TO OPEN GUARD POSTURE CONTROL

A lot of times when an opponent postures up in your guard, he will immediately begin to throw looping punches at your head. In this sequence, I demonstrate how to defend against those punches and establish the open guard posture control position at the same time. Once accomplished, your opponent's ground and pound options will be minimal at best, allowing you to either work back to the standing position or transition into the omaplata position.

Feijao places his hands on my hips and postures up in my closed guard.

As Feijao cocks his right arm back to throw a looping punch, I reach my left hand toward his head and begin to sit up.

As Feijao drops his punch, I open my guard, roll onto my right shoulder, and hook my left hand around the back of his head. To block his strike, I drive my left elbow into his right biceps. Having shifted my head away from my centerline and employed defensive tactics, his fist collides with the back of my left shoulder instead of my face.

Continuing with his assault, Feijao cocks his left arm back and throws a hook toward the right side of my face.

To block Feijao's hook, I catch his left biceps with my right hand. Next, I keep his left arm extended away from his body, slide my right knee underneath his left arm, and place my right foot on his left hip.

Continuing to pull Feijao's head down with my left hand and control his left arm with my right hand, I place my left foot on his right hip and pinch my knees together. To secure open guard posture control, I grab his triceps with my right hand and pin his arm to my right shin. Now that I'm well protected, I will immediately begin setting up an attack.

OPEN GUARD POSTURE CONTROL

GET-UP FROM OPEN GUARD POSTURE CONTROL

Securing open guard posture control stifles your opponent's attacks. To revive his offense, he will often attempt to pull his head upward to create space. In such a situation, you can use his reaction to your advantage by escaping back to your feet using the technique demonstrated below. When studying the photos, you'll notice that I utilize different grips in the two columns. In the left column, I use a left collar tie to aid my escape, and in the right column, I place my left hand on my opponent's shoulder and throat. Both grips allow you to achieve the same goal, which is to maintain distance and prevent your opponent from shooting in and hauling you back to the mat. However, the collar tie keeps you in close range as you climb back to your feet, and placing your hand on your opponent's throat creates more separation as you stand. Deciding which grip to choose should be based on your immediate goals in the fight.

I've secured the open guard posture control position on Feijao.

Feijao forces his head up and attempts to straighten his posture. Instead of resisting, I hang on to his head and use his upward pull to help lift my head and shoulders off the mat.

As Feijao postures, I sit up and post my right elbow on the mat. It is important to notice that in the picture on the left, I maintain control of his head using my left collar tie, but in the photo on the right, I wrap the web of my left hand around the side of his neck and throat.

4a) Keeping my left hand wrapped around the back of Feijao's head, I create distance by driving my right foot into his left hip and scooting my hips backward.

4b) To create distance, I push into Feijao's neck with my left hand, drive my right foot into his left hip, and scoot my hips backward.

5a) Still controlling Feijao's head and driving his hips away from me, I post my right hand on the mat behind me, coil my left leg inward, and elevate my hips.

5b) Continuing to drive my left hand into Feijao's neck and force his hips away from me, I post my right hand on the mat, coil my left leg inward, and elevate my hips.

6

Posting on my left foot and right hand, I slide my right leg underneath my body. Notice how I'm still using my left hand to control distance.

7

I plant my right knee on the mat. Having escaped my body out from underneath Feijao, I can now work back to the standing position.

OMAPLATA TRANSITION WITH SHOULDER-LOCK FINISH

When you establish open guard posture control, you can flow right into the omaplata position. If you are successful with the transition, you have numerous attacking options at your disposal. Deciding which option to chose should be based upon your opponent's reaction to the position. In the sequence below, my opponent offers minimal resistance, allowing me to finish him with the omaplata shoulder-lock submission. This is an extremely effective technique that I use frequently in both training and in fights. I strongly suggest that you give it the attention it deserves.

1

I've secured the open guard posture control position on Feijao.

2

I release my head control and grab Feijao's right wrist with my left hand.

3

Still pinning Feijao's right wrist to my left hip using my left hand, I reach my right arm across my body and grab his right elbow.

4

I break Feijao's posture by pulling his right elbow into my abdomen using my right hand, kicking off his left hip using my right foot, and escaping my hips out from underneath his body. Next, I throw my left leg over his back and position my left foot in front of his left shoulder.

5

Continuing to control Feijao's right arm using both of my hands, I scoot my hips out toward my right side. Next, I slide my right leg out from underneath his body and post my foot on the mat.

I post my right hand on the mat, coil my left leg over Feijao's right shoulder, and begin to sit up. The combination of these actions breaks his posture and forces his head to the mat.

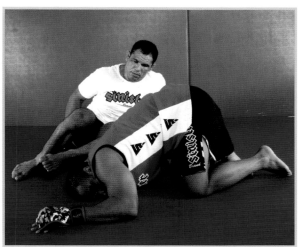

As I apply downward pressure to the back of Feijao's right shoulder using my left leg, I release my left grip on his right arm, post my left hand on the mat, and sit up.

Keeping my left leg coiled around the back of Feijao's right shoulder, I elevate my hips off the mat using my left hand, corkscrew my body in a counterclockwise direction, and plant my right hand on the mat next to Feijao's right leg. The combination of these actions places a tremendous amount of pressure on his shoulder, causing him to tap. It is important to note that by keeping my hips elevated, I distribute more weight over his shoulder, thereby pinning his shoulder to the mat and preventing him from posturing and escaping the submission.

OPEN GUARD POSTURE CONTROL

SEQUENCE A: COUNTER POSTURE DEFENSE

When you apply the omaplata shoulder-lock submission shown in the previous sequence, it's not uncommon for your opponent to posture up in an attempt to escape. In such a scenario, this technique can come in handy. To pull it off, reach your arm over your opponent's body and grab his far hip. Next, draw his body toward you and scoot your hips back, pulling his trapped right arm with you. The combination of these actions will break his posture and force his chest to the mat, allowing you to immediately return to the omaplata shoulder-lock submission. In the photos below I demonstrate how to employ these added steps. If you've forgotten how to finish the submission, revisit the previous sequence.

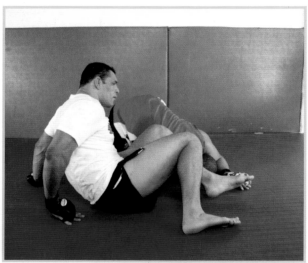

I've trapped Feijao's right arm by securing the omaplata position, and I am preparing to finish him with the shoulder-lock submission.

Before I can corkscrew my body and apply the submission, Feijao drives his left hand off the mat and postures up. The instant he does this, I reach my right arm over his back and grab his far hip.

MASTERING MIXED MARTIAL ARTS

Driving my left leg down into Feijao's right shoulder, I pull his body toward me using my grip on his far hip. Notice how this causes him to fall to his right shoulder.

Continuing to pull Feijao toward me and apply downward pressure to his right shoulder, I scoot my hips back. The combination of these actions causes him to collapse to his right hip. With his posture completely broken, I will immediately transition back to the shoulder-lock submission.

OMAPLATA TO STRAIGHT ARMBAR

Unless your opponent is an inexperienced grappler, the chances are he will attempt some type of escape when you establish the omaplata position. In the previous sequence I demonstrated how to break your opponent back down when he attempts to escape by posturing up, and in this sequence I demonstrate how to transition into a straight armbar when your opponent attempts to defend by straightening his arm. This is a very common escape, making this technique an important one to have in your arsenal. Both my brother Rogerio and I use this transition on a daily basis in training.

I've trapped Feijao's left arm by establishing the omaplata position.

To prevent me from sitting up and securing the shoulder-lock submission, Feijao straightens his left arm across my chest.

Maintaining a firm grip on Feijao's left wrist using my left hand, I drive off my left foot, turn onto my right side, and slide my right leg down the back of his left arm. Notice how I've shifted my hips so that my crotch is lined up with his left elbow.

To trap Feijao's left arm, I place my left leg on top of my right leg and then hook my left foot over my right foot. It is important to note that when making this transition, you must keep your opponent's arm locked tight to your body using your left hand.

To apply the straight armbar, I establish a thumb grip using my left hand, thrust my hips into Feijao's left elbow, and pull his left arm over my left leg using both of my hands. To see the details of the thumb grip, visit page 103.

OMAPLATA SWEEP

If it's late in the fight and both you and your opponent are covered in sweat, it can be difficult to finish him with the omaplata shoulder-lock submission due to the slip factor. In such a situation, an excellent option is to transition from the omaplata into the sweep demonstrated below. As long as you're fluid with your movements, you'll put your opponent on his back and secure the side control position. If you look at the first photo below, you'll notice that I've reversed my open guard posture control. Instead of positioning my right knee in front of my opponent's left shoulder, I've positioned my left knee in front of his right shoulder. Although in the beginning you'll find it easier to continuously go to one side, it is important to eventually learn how to establish control positions and lock in submissions from both sides to keep your opponent guessing. Just as he gets used to defending the right side of his body from your attacks, you switch things up and attack his left side. It's a great way to catch your opponent off guard.

I've established the open guard posture control position on Feijao. Notice how I've switched my control from previous sequences. Here I'm keeping his posture broken with my left hand, and I'm gripping his left wrist with my right hand. Also notice that I've positioned my left knee in front of his right shoulder. Having reversed my control, I will apply the omaplata on his left arm instead of his right.

Using my right hand, I pin Feijao's left wrist to my right hip. Next, I grab his left elbow with my left hand and pull it into my abdomen.

Driving my left foot into Feijao's right hip, I escape my hips out from underneath his body, throw my right leg over his back, and position my right foot in front of his right shoulder.

I slide my left leg out from underneath Feijao's body and then post my left foot on the mat. Next, I push off the mat with my left foot, shrimp my hips toward my left side, turn toward my right side, and wedge my right hand to the inside of Feijao's left leg. It is important to note that I'm applying downward pressure to his back using my right leg and keeping a tight grip on his left elbow using my left hand. The former prevents him from posturing up, and the latter prevents him from escaping his trapped arm.

Still shrimping my hips toward my left side, I wrap my right leg around the back of Feijao's left shoulder, hook my right arm around the inside of his left leg, and grip my hands together.

I pull my arms tight to my body, pinning Feijao's left leg to my right shoulder. Notice how this makes our bodies perfectly parallel. Next, I pinch my knees together and begin rolling toward my left side.

With my knees pinched together and Feijao's left leg pinned to my chest, I roll onto my left shoulder.

I roll over my left shoulder and drive my right knee to the mat.

With Feijao's left arm trapped between my legs, he is unable to post his arm and block the sweep. As he gets forced to his back, I roll up to my right knee.

The instant I come up onto my knees, I release my grip, post my left foot on the mat, and begin sliding my right leg underneath my left leg.

To secure side control, I move my right arm over Feijao's body, drive my right elbow underneath his right arm, sprawl my left leg out to the side, pin my right knee to his left hip, and sit my butt to the mat. To keep his back flat on the mat, I distribute my weight over his torso.

OMAPLATA TO MOUNT

When you establish the omaplata position, your opponent's most common escape will be to execute a forward roll over the shoulder of his trapped arm. Although it's a legitimate escape, it's easily countered using this technique. The instant your opponent rolls, sit up with him, throw your leg over his body, and secure the mount position. The most important element of this technique is timing. If you're slow to react, your opponent will climb to his knees and land in your guard. Once you get the hang of using this maneuver to transition to the mount, practice using it to transition to side control. It's set up the same way, but instead of stepping your leg over his torso, turn into him and throw your near arm over your torso. Both transitions are equally effective. Deciding which one to utilize should boil down to your goals in the fight.

I've secured the omaplata position on Feijao. Notice that I've secured his left wrist with my left hand.

In an attempt to escape the omaplata, Feijao drives off his right foot and initiates a forward roll over his left shoulder.

3

Feijao rolls forward over his left shoulder.

4

As Feijao rolls onto his upper back, I begin to sit up.

5

As Feijao rolls to his back, I post my right hand on the mat and sit up. Notice that I'm still gripping his left wrist with my left hand.

OPEN GUARD POSTURE CONTROL

The moment Feijao's feet hit the mat, I release my left grip on his wrist and begin sliding my left knee across his torso.

I slide my left knee down to the mat on Feijao's right side.

To secure the mount, I hook my legs underneath Feijao's legs, drive my hips into his stomach, and arch my back.

OMAPLATA TO BACK

Sometimes when you establish the omaplata position, your opponent will defend against the shoulder-lock submission but make no real effort to escape. In such a situation, you have a couple of options. You can utilize the sweep to side control transition demonstrated earlier in the book or you can use the technique demonstrated below to take his back. The sweep requires fewer steps, making it more difficult for your opponent to counter, but taking his back gives you more offensive options. Again, deciding which technique to employ boils down to preference and your goals in the fight. In the first sequence below, I show how to secure the back position by establishing an over-under body lock. However, a lot of times when you take your opponent's back he will keep a tight guard to prevent your from establishing your second hook and securing the position. An excellent way to deal with this scenario is to apply a kimura grip on your opponent's far arm and then use your control to create enough space to get your second hook. I demonstrate how this can be accomplished in the following sequence.

I've secured the omaplata position and trapped Feijao's left arm. To prevent him from rolling over his shoulder as I make the transition to his back, I've sat up, wrapped my right arm over his back, and latched onto his far hip with my right hand.

Maintaining downward pressure on Feijao's left shoulder using my right leg, I coil my left leg inward and wedge my left foot underneath his left shoulder.

I slide my left leg underneath Feijao's body and then hook it around the front of his left leg.

Momentarily releasing my right grip on Feijao's right hip, I slide my right leg down his back.

I drop my right leg over Feijao's legs and plant my foot on the mat. At the same time, I quickly reestablish my right grip on his right hip.

Posting on my right foot and left hand, I pull Feijao into me using my right hand, climb up to my left knee, and elevate my hips off the mat.

I climb up onto Feijao's back, hook my left leg around the inside of his left leg, and reach my right arm underneath his right arm.

I wrap my left arm over Feijao's left shoulder and grip my hands together in the center of his chest, forming an over-under lock.

To secure the back position and flatten Feijao's body to the mat, I hook my right leg around the inside of his right leg, sprawl my legs back, and drive my hips into his lower back. From here, I can begin striking the sides of his head or work for a choke.

SEQUENCE A: KIMURA GRIP SECOND HOOK VARIATION

When you take your opponent's back with over-under control, sometimes he will manage to pin his far elbow to his knee to prevent you from securing your second hook. Employing the technique I demonstrate below is a quick remedy for such a situation.

1

In this scenario, Feijao has pinned his right elbow to his right knee to prevent me from hooking my right leg around the inside of his right leg and establishing my second hook.

2

To create the space I need to establish my right hook, I establish a kimura grip on his right arm by grabbing the top of his right wrist with my right hand. Next, I pull his hand underneath his body while driving my right forearm upward into the back of his right shoulder.

3

Having created space, I throw my right leg over Feijao's back.

I slide my right leg to the inside of Feijao's right leg, establishing my second hook.

To secure the back position and flatten Feijao's body to the mat, I sprawl my legs back and drive my hips into his lower back.

I release my grip on Feijao's right wrist, cock my right arm back, and prepare to throw strikes at the side of his head.

INSIDE HOOKS GUARD TRANSITION

Sometimes it can be difficult to lock in the omaplata from open guard posture control, especially when you're up against an experienced grappler. When faced with this dilemma, a good option is to transition to another control position to see if you have any more luck. In the sequence below, I demonstrate how to transition from open guard posture control to the inside hooks guard, a position which arms you with numerous sweeps. The movements involved are similar to the get-up technique I offered earlier in the book in that you drive your foot into your opponent's hip to create space. However, instead of using that space to climb back to your feet, you use it to sit up and secure the inside hooks guard. If you look at the last photo in the sequence, you'll notice that I establish an inside hook and an underhook on the same side of my opponent's body, which allows me to immediately employ offensive techniques. It's also important to notice that I've positioned my head underneath my opponent's head. This is key because it allows me to keep my opponent postured, which in turn allows me to execute a number of highly effective sweeps. To learn the sweeps at your disposal from the inside hooks guard, flip to the section devoted to this position.

1 I've established the open guard posture control position on Feijao.

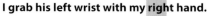

2 I grab his left wrist with my right hand.

To create the space I need to transition to the inside hooks guard, I drive my right foot into Feijao's left hip, roll onto my right hip, and scoot my butt back. When executing these movements, it is important to that you control your opponent's head and arm to prevent him from posturing up and throwing strikes.

As I slide my hips back, I move my left foot in front of Feijao's right leg.

I hook my left foot to the inside of Feijao's right leg.

6

Maintaining a strong right grip on Feijao's left wrist, I release my grip on his head and begin driving my left hand to the inside of his right arm.

7

I slide my right foot to the inside of Feijao's right leg, wedge my left hand underneath his right arm, and begin to sit up. Notice how I'm driving my left leg upward into Feijao's right leg—this action turns my left leg into an anchor, making it easier for me to sit up.

8

Maintaining tight control of Feijao's left wrist using my right hand, I wrap my left arm around his back and post on my right elbow. To secure the inside hook guard, I position my head underneath Feijao's chin and to the right of his head. From here, I will immediately transition into a sweep.

DOUBLE WRIST CONTROL CLOSED GUARD

DOUBLE ARM CONTROL OPEN GUARD

As you now know, the best way to defend against your opponent's attacks and still remain on the offensive is to secure one of the posture control guards demonstrated in the previous section. By gluing your body to your opponent's body, you eliminate the space he needs to strike. However, sometimes when you reach a posture control position, your opponent will realize any action he makes will only allow you to better set up an attack. Instead of attempting to strike or pass your guard, he focuses all his energy on defending against your attacks. If you should find yourself in such a stalemate, transitioning to double wrist control closed guard or double arm control open guard can be a good way to get your offense going. In this portion of the section I show submissions that can be applied from both, but it is important to remember that you are better protected and have a lot more options from the various posture control positions. If you transition to one of the double arm controls and fail to submit your opponent, and he becomes active again, you want to immediately transition back to a posture control position.

DOUBLE WRIST CONTROL CLOSED GUARD

In this section you will learn my favorite attack from the double wrist control closed guard—

the triangle. It's possible to set up other sub-missions from this position, such as armbars and omaplatas, but I prefer to utilize those sub-missions from the posture control positions. Continuing with the theme of the book, I've also included several methods of dealing with your opponent's defenses to the triangle.

DOUBLE ARM CONTROL OPEN GUARD

The double arm control open guard position is similar to open guard posture control in that you are sitting up and have both of your feet positioned on your opponent's hips. However, instead of gaining control of his head using one hand and establishing inside control with the other, you wrap both of your arms around the outside of his arms, which hinders him from punching and backing out of your guard. From this position, I demonstrate how to execute the arm drag and the arm drag variation, both of which are used to take your opponent's back.

TRIANGLE CHOKE

The triangle is the first submission I'll attempt when I secure double wrist control on my opponent. It's a common submission in MMA, but it would be responsible for a lot more victories if competitors took the time to master the small details that make the triangle so effective. I've outlined these details in the sequence below, and studying them thoroughly should dramatically increase your success with this submission. However, utilizing proper form is just half the battle. You must also learn how to deal with your opponent's defensive tactics. If your opponent defends against the triangle by climbing to his feet or posturing up, you have a couple of options. You can counter by locking in an armbar (sequence A), or you can make a quick transition to the mount (sequence B).

Technical Note: To secure wrist control, most fighters will grab their opponent's wrist with their entire hand and cinch down as forcefully as they can. This is totally unnecessary. If you look at the bone structure of the human wrist, you will see that there is a narrow gap where the small bones of the wrist meet the large bones of the forearm. Establishing a grip in this gap provides the best control. The gap is far too small to fit an entire hand; however, it is the perfect size to fit your middle finger and thumb. Although it might not seem like you can establish a firm grip with just two fingers, give it a try and I guarantee you'll be pleasantly surprised. If you're fighting in MMA, you can secure an even tighter grip. Examine an MMA glove and you will see that there is a gap between the strap that covers the wrist and the pad that covers the top of the hand. When you wrap your middle finger and thumb around that gap, the padding serves as a backstop that prevents your grip from slipping down your opponent's hand. I'm not saying that you want to keep your other fingers extended as through you were drinking tea out of fine china—they should still be wrapped around your opponent's wrist—but the majority of squeezing should be done with your middle finger and thumb. When you utilize this form of wrist control, your opponent will have a much harder time breaking your grip. In addition to this, you save loads of grip strength, which means you can hang on for a lot longer before burning out your arms.

Feijao is postured up in my closed guard with his hands posted on my hips. To force a reaction, I establish double wrist control by grabbing his wrists with my hands.

To set up the triangle, I cross Feijao's right arm toward my left side and his left arm toward my right side. This action not only forces him off balance, but it will force him to react in such a way that will allow me to further set up the triangle. It is important to notice that I crossed his left arm over his right arm.

As Feijao reacts to my previous action by pulling his arms toward his body, I push his right arm to the inside of my left leg using my left hand. At the same time, I grab the back of his head using my right hand. It is important to note that if I had crossed his right arm over his left arm, instead of the other way around, I would have forced his left arm to the inside of my right leg using my right hand. It is also important to notice that once I grab the back of his head with my right hand, I use that control to keep his posture broken down. If you allow your opponent to posture up, there is a good chance he will escape as you open your guard to lock in the triangle.

Continuing to drive Feijao's right arm downward using my left hand and controlling his posture using my right hand, I open my guard and throw my legs toward the front of his shoulders.

I wrap my left leg over Feijao's right shoulder and across the back of his neck. Next, I hook my left foot underneath my right foot, trapping his left arm and head between my legs. Notice how I'm still controlling his posture using my right hand.

I grab Feijao's left wrist with my left hand and then pull his arm toward the left side of my body.

With Feijao's left arm stretched across my abdomen, I pin his left hand to my left hip using my grip on his wrist.

DOUBLE ARM CONTROL

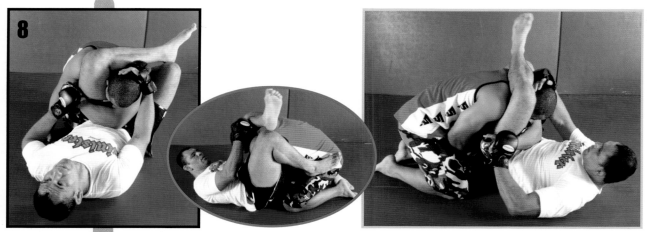

8

I place my right foot on Feijao's left hip and push off. At the same time, I escape my hips toward my right side and wrap my left leg over the back of his neck. Notice how throughout these steps I have continued to pin his left hand to my left hip and maintain control of his posture using my grip on the back of his head.

9

Releasing my head control, I grab my left shin with my right hand. This action not only helps prevent Feijao from posturing up, but it also keeps my left leg positioned across the back of his neck.

10

I hook the crook of my right leg over the top of my left foot.

I curl my right leg downward, forcing my left leg into the back of Feijao's head. I add additional downward pressure by pulling my left shin toward my body using my right hand. To finish the triangle submission, I squeeze everything tight.

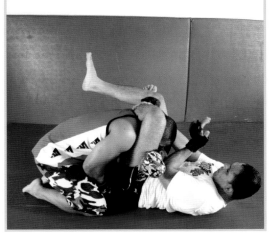

Feijao refuses to tap to the triangle, so I must make my hold tighter by pulling his head toward my abdomen using both of my hands. To begin this task, I grab the back of his head with my right hand and release my left grip on his left wrist. However, the instant I release my left grip, his first reaction is to pull his trapped arm toward the right side of my body. If he can accomplish this goal, his left shoulder will no longer be digging into his carotid artery, rendering the submission useless. To prevent this from happening, I drive my left elbow into his left arm to keep him from pulling it free.

With Feijao's left arm trapped to his neck, I place my left hand on the back of his head. To finish the submission, I pull his head down with both of my hands and squeeze my legs tight.

SEQUENCE A: TRIANGLE TO ARMBAR FINISH

When you throw your leg over your opponent's shoulder and lock in the triangle choke, he will most likely sense danger and attempt to escape. If the triangle is tight and he's unable to posture up, one of his only viable options is to quickly climb to his feet and attempt to pull his head and trapped arm free from your lock. In such a situation, you no longer have the weight of his body stacking you in your guard, making it easy to straighten his arm and apply an armbar. Your opponent will undoubtedly attempt to resist the submission, but with it being a battle between your entire body and the muscles in his arm, you will almost always win. I submitted Mark Coleman with this exact technique when we fought in the Pride Fighting Championships. I caught him in a triangle, he climbed to his feet to break my lock, and I utilized his escape to lock in the armbar. As I have already mentioned, having the ability to transition from one submission to the next based upon your opponent's reactions is critical in MMA competition.

I've captured Feijao's left arm and head between my legs, and I'm working to finish him with a triangle choke.

To combat the triangle, Feijao posts his right foot on the mat and begins to stand up.

3

As Feijao posts his left foot on the mat and stands up, I grab his left wrist with both of my hands and straighten his arm across the length of my chest. To prevent his escaping the submission, I keep my legs locked tight and maintain a tight squeeze on his head and trapped arm.

4

I wrap my left thumb around Feijao's left thumb and then wrap my other fingers around the outside of his thumb and the top of his hand. Next, I wrap my right hand over my left hand. Once I have properly secured control of his left arm, I finish the arm-bar by twisting his left arm over my right hip, elevating my hips into his elbow, and squeezing my knees together. It is important to mention that I'm still curling my right leg down into my left leg to apply pressure to the back of Feijao's head. This prevents him from further straightening his posture, pulling his head free, and escaping the submission.

TECHNICAL NOTE: When you apply an armbar, your opponent will most likely twist his arm in every direction in an attempt to avoid the submission. If you don't have a controlling grip on his arm, finishing the armbar can be difficult to manage. To combat this defense, I will always employ the grip shown here. By wrapping your thumb around the inside of your opponent's thumb and your fingers over the top of his thumb and hand, you can control and manipulate the positioning of his arm with ease. If you look at the close-up, you'll also notice that I reinforce this grip using my opposite hand, giving me even more control. If you get confused as to which hand has which task, follow this rule—If you have your opponent's left arm trapped, form your main grip around his thumb using your left hand. If you have his right arm trapped, form your main grip around his thumb using your right hand. When you master this grip, you will dramatically increase your finishing percentage.

SEQUENCE B: TRIANGLE TO MOUNT

If your opponent senses the triangle coming before you have a chance lock the hold tight and control his posture, he will often attempt to escape the submission by positioning his knees underneath your butt, lifting his head toward the sky, and posturing up. Although it can be very difficult to assume the leg positioning needed to finish the choke with his knees tucked under your backside, his base is extremely weak from this position, allowing you to transition from the triangle to a sweep that takes you to the mount. Once in the mount, you can then work to reposition your legs and finish the triangle choke from the top position.

I've trapped Feijao's right arm and head between my legs and I'm working to finish a triangle choke.

Before I can position my right leg across the back of Feijao's neck to control his posture and cinch in the choke, he digs his knees underneath my butt, lifts his head, and postures up. From here, he is in an excellent position from which to defend the triangle. However, the position compromises his base, making him vulnerable to being swept. Instead of trying to fight a losing battle, I decide to capitalize on his weakened base by transitioning from the triangle choke to a sweep.

As Feijao postures up, I post my right hand on the mat behind my head, elevate my hips, push off my posted right hand, and turn toward my left side. There are a couple of small details you must pay special attention to. Notice how I'm maintaining tight control of Feijao's right arm to prevent him from posting his right hand on the mat and blocking the sweep. Also notice how I have my guard closed and my knees pinched together. If you fail with either, you will not only lose the sweep, but also the triangle submission.

Keeping a tight grip on Feijao's right wrist, I continue to elevate my hips, push off the mat with my right hand, and turn toward my left side. With Feijao's knees positioned underneath my butt, his base is weak and he begins to fall.

I come down onto my left side and roll over my left shoulder. Unable to post his right hand on the mat and block the sweep, Feijao falls to his right side.

6

Continuing with my roll, I release my left grip on Feijao's right wrist.

7

As Feijao is swept to his back, I post my right hand and right knee on the mat to establish a solid base. Next, I straighten my left leg, reach my left hand underneath my left leg, and then grab my right instep with my left hand. It is important to mention that what made these steps possible is the fact that I rolled up onto my right knee. If you fail to do this, the weight of your body will pin your opponent's body on top of your right leg, making it very difficult for you to grab your right instep and pull your foot behind the crook of your left leg.

8

Using my left hand, I pull my right foot upward and position it in the crook of my left leg. Next, I release my left grip on my foot and grab the back of Feijao's head with my left hand. To finish the triangle from the mount position, I pull his head off the mat using my left hand, squeeze my knees together, curl my left leg up into my right foot, and drive my hips into the back of his right arm.

ARM DRAG FROM OPEN GUARD

In this sequence, I demonstrate how to execute a basic arm drag from the open guard. The best time to employ this technique is when your opponent drives his weight forward into your guard. Before he has a chance to pull his weight away, you sit up, isolate one of his arms by establishing the arm drag position, and then pull his arm across your body. When done properly and at the right moment, he will fall forward and plant his free hand on the mat. This gives you several options. You can use his compromised positioning to execute a Darse choke (sequence A) or you can transition to his back (sequence B). With both options, commitment is the key to success. In a split second, you must assess the situation and then go for one option or the other. If there is any hesitation, your chance of locking in a submission or transitioning to a more dominant position drops dramatically.

Technical Note: It is important to notice my starting position in the sequence below. When my opponent is active in my guard, the majority of the time I will establish one of the posture control positions described in this book. However, if my opponent is inactive in my guard, I will often open my guard and assume control of his arms. Previously I demonstrated double wrist control, and in this sequence I demonstrate double arm control.

Feijao is driving his weight forward into my open guard. Notice how I have both of my knees positioned in front of his biceps, my feet are on his hips, and I'm gripping the back of his arms with my hands.

As Feijao drives his weight forward, I push off his right hip with my left foot and scoot my hips toward my left side. At the same time, I slide my left hand down his right arm, grab his right wrist with my left hand, slide my right leg between his legs, and hook my right foot around the inside of his right leg.

Removing my left foot from Feijao's right hip, I sit up, push his right hand toward my right side using my left hand, dive my right arm underneath his right arm, and cup the fingers of my right hand around his triceps just below his shoulder.

Having established the arm drag position, I pull Feijao's right arm toward my right side. Fluid with my movements, he falls forward and posts his right hand on the mat. From here, I can either execute a Darse choke (sequence A) or transition to his back (sequence B).

SEQUENCE A: ARM DRAG TO DARSE CHOKE

In this sequence, I've executed an arm drag from the open guard, causing my opponent to lurch forward and place his free hand on the mat. To capitalize on his positioning, I immediately transition to the Darse choke.

I've pulled Feijao off balance using the arm drag. Instead of transitioning to his back, I decide to apply the Darse submission.

Controlling Feijao's right arm with my right arm to keep his posture broken, I dive my left arm underneath his right arm.

3

I wedge my left arm underneath Feijao's chin so that the inside of my wrist is cutting into the left side of his neck. Next, I grip my hands together palm-to-palm on the left side of his neck. Once my grip is secure, I drive my right forearm down into the back of his head.

4

Having forced Feijao's head down, I unclasp my hands and straighten my right arm. It is important to notice that I'm straightening my right arm underneath my left hand and above his head. Not only does this position his head in my armpit, but it will also allow me to grab my right biceps with my left hand and secure a figure-four lock with my arms. However, it is very important to force your opponent's head down using the previous step before attempting to apply the figure-four. If you fail to do this, you most likely won't be able to finish the submission.

5

I establish the figure-four lock by grabbing my right biceps with my left hand and placing my right hand on the back of Feijao's left shoulder. To finish the Darse choke, I use my figure-four lock to pull Feijao's body into me. This drives his right shoulder into the right side of his neck and drives my left arm into the left side of his neck, cutting off the blood flow to his brain.

SEQUENCE B: ARM DRAG TO BACK TRANSITION

Once again I have utilized an arm drag from the open guard, causing my opponent to lurch forward and place his free hand on the mat, but instead of applying the Darse submission as I did in the previous sequence, I decide to transition to his back and apply a rear choke. It is important to pay special attention to the last few steps because I finish the submission differently than most. Instead of applying a figure-four lock around my opponent's neck, which would allow him to grab my lever arm and reposition it over his head, I clasp my hands together and position my lever arm behind his shoulder, eliminating such a defense. To better illustrate the nuances of the choke, I've provided an alternate angle in sequence B1.

I've utilized an arm drag from open guard, causing Feijao to fall forward and place his free hand on the mat.

The instant I pull Feijao off balance, I post my right hand on the mat, reach my left arm over his back, and cup my left hand around his waist just above his far hip. To prevent him from rolling to his back and putting me in his guard, I use my grip on his hip to pull his body into me.

3

Driving off the mat using my right hand and left foot, I climb up to my right knee. At the same time, I wedge my left hand to the inside of his left leg. Not only does this anchor help me pull myself up onto his back, but it also allows me to keep his hips pinned to mine.

4

I slide my left arm underneath Feijao's left arm and then grab the top of his wrist with my left hand.

5

To flatten Feijao's body toward the mat and create the space I need to establish my second hook, I pull his left arm underneath his body using my left hand.

6

Having created the space I need to get my second hook, I throw my left leg over Feijao's back.

7

I hook my left foot around the inside of Feijao's left leg, securing my second hook. To flatten his body to the mat, I sprawl my legs back and drive my hips into his lower back.

8

The instant I break Feijao down, I cock my right arm back.

I land a right hook to the right side of Feijao's jaw.

Having opened space between Feijao's chin and chest with my punch, I dig my right hand underneath his body and slide my forearm across his neck.

I wrap my right arm around Feijao's neck and then clasp my hands together using a specialized grip. My right palm is facing downward, and the top of my left hand is flush with his left shoulder. To finish the choke, I drive my left forearm into the back of his left shoulder, which allows me to draw my right arm tight around his neck. To add additional pressure to the choke, I press my head down into the back of his head.

SEQUENCE B1: REAR CHOKE

In this sequence, I demonstrate the rear choke from an alternate position so you can better understand how it is applied.

I've secured control of Feijao's back. I have my left arm wrapped underneath his left arm, and I'm gripping the top of his left wrist with my left hand. This control allows me to pin his left arm to his body, which prevents him from defending against the choke.

I land a punch to the right side of Feijao's jaw to create space between his chin and chest. Before he can close that space, I drive my right thumb underneath the right side of his jaw.

I drive my right fist across Feijao's neck, forcing his chin to his left. This opens an even bigger space between his chin and chest, which allows me to slide my right forearm across his neck. When executing this step, it is important to keep your hand closed in a fist. If you open your hand, your opponent can grip your fingers and peel your hand away.

Wrapping my right arm around Feijao's neck, I grip the back of his left shoulder with my right hand.

I release my grip on Feijao's left wrist and then grab the outside of my right hand using my left hand. Notice how my right palm is facing down, and the top of my left hand is flush with his shoulder.

To finish the choke, I drive my left forearm into the back of Feijao's left shoulder. This serves as a fulcrum and allows me to pull my right arm tight around his neck. To add even more pressure to the choke, I press my head down into the back of his head.

TEN-FINGER GRIP ARM DRAG TO BACK TRANSITION

In previous sequences, I demonstrated how to execute an arm drag when your opponent drives his weight forward into your open guard. Now I demonstrate how to execute an arm drag when he sits his weight back and stalls in your open guard. Since he's not giving you any energy to counter, you establish a ten-finger grip on his arm, force his weight forward, and then transition to his back. When studying the photos, pay special attention to the direction that I drag my opponent's isolated arm. Instead of dragging it across my body as I did in the previous arm drag techniques, I trap his arm between my legs. This makes it very difficult for my opponent to defend against the rear choke when I take his back.

Feijao is in my open guard, sitting his weight back. Notice that I've positioned my knees in front of his biceps, placed my feet on his hips, and gripped the back of his arms with my hands. Since he's stalling in my guard, I decide to use the ten-finger grip arm drag to transition to his back.

To secure the ten-finger grip arm drag position, I sit up, wedge my right hand underneath Feijao's right armpit, wrap my left arm around the outside of his right shoulder, and then grip my hands together behind his right arm. Notice how the back of my right hand is flush with the back of his arm. Assuming this grip will allow me to use both hands to drag his body forward.

Leaning my weight back, I pull Feijao's right shoulder toward my right, slide my right leg between his legs, and extend my left leg to the outside of his right leg. At the same time, I pull his right arm to the inside of my left leg, allowing me to capture it between my legs.

As I continue to pull Feijao's right shoulder toward my right side, I sit up and rotate my body in a clockwise direction. Due to the explosiveness of my movements, his head is forced to the mat.

As I sit up, I release my grip behind Feijao's right arm. This allows me to post my right hand on the mat, reach my left arm over his back, and cup my left hand around his waist just above his left hip. The instant I establish this grip, I pull Feijao's body into me to prevent him from rolling to his back and establishing the guard position.

6

Driving off the mat using my right hand and left foot, I climb up to my right knee. Notice how I have trapped Feijao's right arm using my right leg. Next, I dive my left arm underneath his left arm and grab the top of his wrist with my left hand. Assuming this control will prevent him from pinning his left elbow to his left knee and eliminating the space I need to establish my second hook.

7

I throw my left leg over Feijao's back.

8

I hook my left foot around the inside of Feijao's left leg. To flatten his body out on the mat, I sprawl my legs back and drive my hips into his lower back. From here, I can immediately work to finish him with a rear choke.

SEQUENCE A: ROLLING TO YOUR BACK

It's usually best to try and finish your opponent with the rear choke from the back mount position, but if he should roll you to your back in an attempt to escape, maintain your control over his body and finish the choke from your new position. As long as you keep his arm trapped underneath your leg, it will be very difficult for him to defend against the submission. To see the finish to the rear choke, revisit the arm drag to back transition, sequence B1.

I've secured control of Feijao's back. I'm trapping his right arm to his body using my right leg, and I'm controlling his left arm with my left hand. My goal is to apply the rear choke and force him to tap.

In an attempt to escape, Feijao rolls over his left shoulder. To prevent him from escaping my control, I keep my legs coiled tight around his body and maintain my left grip on his left wrist.

As Feijao forces me to my back, I maintain the same control.

I land on my back with the same control I started with. From here, I will work to finish him with the rear choke just as I would have from the back mount position.

INSIDE HOOKS GUARD: ANGLE ONE

INSIDE HOOKS GUARD: ANGLE TWO

INSIDE HOOKS GUARD: ANGLE THREE

The inside hooks guard, which is often referred to as butterfly guard, is designed for executing sweeps. However, to be effective from the position you must follow some general rules. The first rule is to sit up into your opponent. If you're lying flat on your back, executing the sweeps offered in this section will be difficult to manage. The second rule is to position your head underneath your opponent's chin and to the opposite side of your underhook. This prevents your opponent from driving his head into your head and nullifying your attacks by flattening your back to the mat. The third rule is to establish an underhook on the same side as your inside hook. For example, if you have your left foot hooked to the inside of your opponent's right leg, you want to secure an underhook using your left arm. The fourth rule is to secure control of your opponent's opposite arm using either an overhook or wrist control. This prevents him from posting that hand on the mat to block your sweeps. The fifth and final rule is to use your control to pull your opponent forward so that his weight is resting on his knees. If you allow him to position his weight over his heels, pulling off a sweep will be nearly impossible to manage. Once you establish the position and have all the rules checked off on your mental list, you can immediately get your offense going by executing the inside hook sweep. Sometimes you'll be successful with it, and other times your opponent will counter. If he counters, you'll want to use his defense to immediately transition into the arm crank inside hook sweep or the guillotine control reverse sweep. Again, the idea is to never stop attacking.

INSIDE HOOK SWEEP TO SIDE CONTROL

Any time I transition to the inside hooks guard from open guard posture control (see page 92) or another position, I will immediately attempt the simple yet effective sweep demonstrated in the sequence below. In order for the sweep to work, you must first disrupt your opponent's base by pulling him into you, which is a detail a lot of fighters tend to forget. If you allow your opponent to keep his center of gravity positioned over his heels, he will have a solid base and most likely be able to block the sweep. In this particular scenario, I use the sweep to transition into side control, but it can also be used to transition into the mount. The only difference with the latter is you stay tighter to your opponent as he goes over. Personally, I feel that side control is a better position for pinning your opponent to the mat, and the mount is a better position for causing damage and landing hard strikes. Deciding which transition to make boils down to your goals in the fight. I strongly suggest drilling this technique as much as possible. Even if your opponent manages to block the sweep by posting his arm or leg on the mat, there are multiple counters you can employ, all of which are covered in this section.

1 I've secured the inside hooks guard on Feijao. Notice my positioning. I've gripped his left wrist with my right hand, established a deep left underhook, hooked my left foot to the inside of his right leg, and coiled my right leg underneath my left leg. To prevent him from flattening my body to the mat, I've positioned my head underneath his chin and to the right of his head. And to hinder him from posturing up, I've pulled his body forward so his weight is on his knees rather than over his heels. From here, I can immediately employ the inside hook sweep.

2 Falling toward my right side, I pull Feijao into me using my left underhook and push his left wrist into his body using my right hand.

INSIDE HOOKS GUARD

SWEEPS

Rolling onto my right side, I push his left arm to the inside of his left thigh using my right hand and elevate his right leg off the mat using my left foot. If you fail to force your opponent's arm underneath his leg, he will be able to post his hand on the mat and block the sweep.

Continuing to roll over my right shoulder and elevate Feijao's right leg, I sweep him toward his back.

As Feijao gets swept to his back, I follow him over, plant my left knee on this stomach, use my right underhook to pin him on his back, and drop my head to the mat. All these steps are extremely important. If you give up space or fail to keep your opponent's back flat on the mat, he will have the room he needs to scramble and possibly reverse his positioning.

INSIDE HOOKS GUARD   123

Using my weight to keep Feijao's shoulders pinned to the mat, I slide my right hand down his left arm and grip his triceps. At the same time, I post my right foot on the mat and begin sliding my left leg underneath my right leg.

I transition into side control by sliding my left leg underneath my posted right leg.

To secure side control, I pull Feijao's left arm off the mat using my right hand, slide my left knee underneath his left shoulder, and drop my hips to the mat. It is important to note that I've kept my weight distributed over his torso throughout the latter part of this transition to prevent him from scrambling and reversing his position.

INSIDE HOOK SWEEP TO MOUNT

In this sequence I demonstrate how to obtain the mount position using the inside hook sweep. When making this transition, your opponent will most likely bridge and attempt to use the momentum of the sweep to force you over to your back. To prevent such an outcome, it is important to hook your legs underneath his legs and immediately stabilize the mount position.

I've secured the inside hooks guard on Feijao. Notice my positioning. I've gripped his left wrist with my right hand, established a deep left underhook, hooked my left foot to the inside of his right leg, and coiled my right leg underneath my left leg. To prevent him from flattening my body to the mat, I've positioned my head underneath his chin and to the right of his head. And to hinder him from posturing up, I've pulled his body forward so his weight is on his knees rather than over his heels. From here, I can immediately employ the inside hook sweep.

Falling toward my right side, I pull Feijao into me using my left underhook and push his left wrist into his body using my right hand.

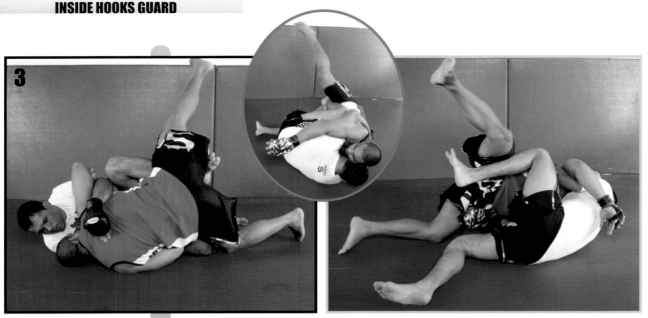

Rolling onto my right side, I push his left arm to the inside of his left thigh using my right hand and elevate his right leg off the mat using my left foot. If you fail to force your opponent's arm underneath his leg, he will be able to post his hand on the mat and block the sweep.

As I sweep Feijao to his back, I obtain the mount position by staying tight to his body and guiding his right leg to the mat using my left foot. Notice how I have ripped my left arm out from underneath his right arm. This prevents him from over-hooking my arm, bridging over his right shoulder, and putting me on my back.

To stabilize the mount position, I hook my feet underneath Feijao's legs, post my right hand on the mat above his left shoulder, and drive my weight forward to pin his shoulders to the mat. Each of these steps is very important because they allow you to stabilize the position. If you fail to control your opponent's body in this manner, he can use the momentum of the sweep to his advantage by bridging over his right shoulder and putting you on your back.

ARM CRANK INSIDE HOOK SWEEP TO SIDE CONTROL

Sometimes when you utilize the inside hook sweep, your opponent will free his trapped arm and block the sweep by posting his hand on the mat. In such a situation, you can use his defense to your advantage by transitioning to the arm crank inside hook sweep. The key to success is speed. If you allow your opponent time to adjust his positioning, he can counter the sweep by posturing up.

I've secured the inside hooks guard on Feijao. Notice my positioning. I've gripped his left wrist with my right hand, established a deep left underhook, hooked my left foot to the inside of his right leg, and coiled my right leg underneath my left leg. To prevent him from flattening my body to the mat, I've positioned my head underneath his chin and to the right of his head. And to hinder him from posturing up, I've pulled his body forward so his weight is on his knees rather than over his heels. From here, I can immediately employ the inside hook sweep.

As I attempt to execute the inside hook sweep, Feijao counters by freeing his trapped arm and posting his hand on the mat.

SWEEPS

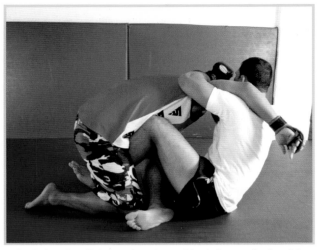

The instant Feijao posts his hand on the mat, I move my head to the left side of his head and trap his right arm by hooking my left arm around the back of his right shoulder.

Without hesitating, I hook my right hand around the back of Feijao's head, grab my right wrist with my left hand, and then use my lock to force his head downward.

Using my grip, I force Feijao's head underneath his body and begin falling toward my right side.

As I fall to my right side, I elevate Feijao's right leg using my left inside hook. Since I'm still driving his head underneath his body with my arms, this action forces him into a forward roll.

Continuing to elevate Feijao's right leg with my left foot, I roll over my right shoulder and force Feijao toward his back.

As Feijao rolls toward his back, I keep my body close to his. From here, I have the option of transitioning into either side control or mount. In this case, I have decided to move into side control.

SWEEPS

Feijao lands on his back and I claim side control. To begin securing the position, I use my left underhook to help pin his shoulders to the mat, post my right foot off to the side, and begin sliding my left leg underneath my right leg. It is important to remember to close off all space and keep your opponent's back pinned to the mat when making this transition. If you fail to do either, he can scramble and possibly reverse his position.

As I move my left leg underneath my posted right leg, I slide my right hand down Feijao's left arm and grip his triceps.

To secure the side control position, I pull Feijao's left arm off the mat using my right hand, slide my left knee underneath his left shoulder, and keep my weight distributed over his torso.

GUILLOTINE CONTROL REVERSE SWEEP

When you execute the inside hook sweep, your opponent has a couple of options to counter. In the previous sequence I demonstrated how to transition into the arm crank inside hook sweep when he counters by placing his hand on the mat, and in this sequence I show how to transition into the guillotine control reverse sweep when he counters by posting his foot on the mat. To be successful with this technique, you must secure a solid grip on your opponent's chin to prevent him from popping his head free and posturing up. I strongly suggest mastering this technique. When performed correctly, you not only put your opponent on his back, but you also assume a position where you can immediately finish the fight with a submission.

I've secured the inside hooks guard on Feijao. Notice my positioning. I've grabbed his left wrist with my right hand, established a deep left underhook, hooked my left foot to the inside of his right leg, and coiled my right leg underneath my left leg. To prevent him from flattening my body to the mat, I've positioned my head underneath his chin and to the right of his head. From here, I can immediately employ the inside hook sweep.

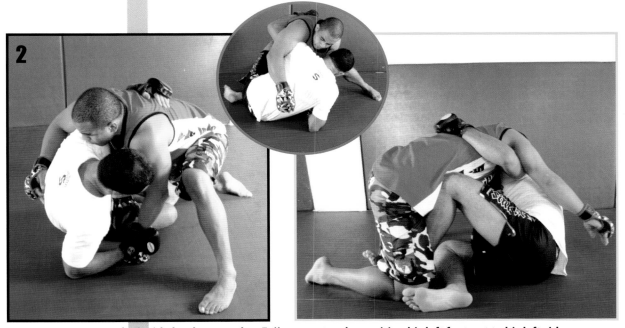

I attempt to execute the inside hook sweep, but Feijao counters by positing his left foot out to his left side.

SWEEPS

The instant Feijao posts his left foot on the mat, I release my underhook and reach my left arm to the left side of his head. Notice how I am still controlling his left wrist with my right hand to prevent him from posturing up and backing out of my guard.

I wrap my left arm around the back of Feijao's head, slide my thumb under his jaw, and cup his chin in my hand.

Maintaining a strong grip on Feijao's chin, I fall toward my right side and hook my right arm underneath his left leg.

Still gripping Feijao's chin, I elevate his right leg using my left foot. At the same time, I begin rolling toward my left side.

7

As Feijao rolls forward over his head, I drop my left leg toward the mat and turn toward my left side. It's important to note that I have maintained a tight grip on his chin and kept my right arm hooked around the inside of his left leg.

8

As Feijao lands on his right side, I continue to rotate my body to claim the top position. With my left hand cupped around his chin and my right arm hooked around his left leg, it is very difficult for him to scramble and escape the position.

In order to pin Feijao's shoulders to the mat, I need to secure a right underhook on his left arm. To accomplish this, I release control of his left leg, flatten my right palm against my chest, and then dig my right arm underneath his left arm. At the same time, I twist my body and move my right leg over my left leg. It is important to note that I'm still gripping his chin with my left hand.

To finish the choke, I twist my hips in a counterclockwise direction and put all of my weight onto Feijao's chest. Notice how this action pulls his head down into his body and drives the inside of my left wrist into his throat. If he doesn't quickly tap, he will pass out.

Many of my victories in MMA competition can be attributed to the work I put into developing my half guard game. As you will see in this section, the position provides you with numerous options. You can transition to your opponent's back, reverse the position with a sweep, and even catch your opponent in a submission. As long as you follow one rule, you can constantly be on the attack.

The one golden rule is simple—NEVER LET YOUR OPPONENT PIN YOUR BACK TO THE MAT! If it seemed like I just screamed that in your face, I'm sorry. I was just trying to get a point across. If you allow your opponent to pin your shoulders by dropping his weight on your chest, he has all sorts of options and you have very few. To prevent this from happening, I demonstrate how to create space and get onto your side using the cross-face and hip block technique. Once accomplished, you have a couple of options. You can execute one of the techniques I show from the cross-face and hip block position, or you can use the space between you and your opponent to secure an underhook, which leads to a slew of attacks. Although these are the two dominant positions from which you will want to attack from the half guard, I also demonstrate how to reverse your position should your opponent succeed in pinning your back to the mat.

As with all types of guards, it is very important not to stall when you have an opponent in your half guard. Whether you secure an un-derhook or are stuck flat on your back, you must constantly move to create a reaction out of your opponent. As you will see, it is your opponent's reaction to your initial movement that allows you to set up the majority of techniques in this section. This of course takes good timing and sensitivity, which is why I recommend drilling the techniques I offer as much as possible. The better you get at stringing techniques together, the more success you'll have from the half guard. And the more success you have, the more fun you'll have playing this vastly under-rated position.

UNDERHOOK CONTROL

When my opponent allows me to get up to my side or I force my way up to my side using the cross-face and hip block technique, I will immediately work to secure an underhook. If successful, it becomes very difficult for my opponent to drive his weight into me and flatten my back to the mat, land effective strikes, or pass my guard into a dominant position. The result is that I remain mobile, which opens up several attacking options. If you look over this section, you'll notice that the majority of techniques are based upon my opponent's reaction to either the underhook control position or my first attack from the position. In most cases, he will wrap his arm around my underhook to form a tight whizzer and then attempt to use that control to drive my body back to the mat. As you will soon see, there are a multitude of techniques that can be used to combat this reaction and set up an attack.

CROSS-FACE AND HIP CONTROL

There are countless reasons why you would choose to initiate an attack from the cross-face and hip control position. For example, if your opponent is driving his weight over your near arm, it can be difficult to dive your arm to the inside of his arm and secure an underhook. In such a situation, employing an offensive technique directly from the cross-face and hip control position is your best chance of getting the upper hand. In this section, I show all of the attacks that I use from this crucial half guard position.

TROUBLESHOOTING THE HALF GUARD

When you have an opponent in your half guard, the goal is to get up onto your side and then execute an offensive technique from either the cross-face and hip block position or from the underhook control position. This is ideal, but not always possible. If your opponent manages to secure an over-under body lock and he drives his shoulder into your jaw, creating space and getting up to your side can be a nearly impossible feat. In such a situation, you need to turn to some alternate methods of escape, and that is what I offer you in this portion of the section. In addition to this, you will also learn how to counter your opponent's attempts to pass your half guard into side control. If you don't understand how to deal with either of these scenarios, your half guard game will have a serious chink in its armor.

SECURING THE CROSS-FACE AND HIP BLOCK POSITION

When in the bottom half guard position, your opponent will often pin your back to the mat by securing an underhook on your far arm and dropping his weight down on your torso. Not only does this eliminate several of your attacking options, but it also puts him in a position where he can easily pass your guard into a more dominant position such as side control or mount. It's in your best interest to prevent this from happening, but if you should find yourself in such a scenario, this is an excellent technique to utilize to create separation between your bodies and get up onto your side. Once you escape your hips out from underneath your opponent, you have several attacking options, many of which I will cover over the coming pages.

1

Feijao is in my half guard. He has established an underhook on my left arm and dropped his weight down onto my torso to pin my back to the mat. Before I can get offensive, I must first create space between our bodies and get up onto my side. Since I have his right leg trapped between my legs, I slide my left arm in front of his face and then grind the outside of my forearm across the right side of his jaw, a technique known as a cross-face. At the same time, I post my right hand on his left hip and then force his hips toward my feet. The combination of these two actions takes a large portion of his weight off my chest.

2

Continuing to drive Feijao's head upward using my cross-face and forcing his hips toward my legs with my right hand, I create enough space between our bodies to begin turning onto my right side.

3

Continuing to create space with the cross-face and hip block, I shrimp my hips toward my left and turn onto my right side. Once I escape my body out from underneath Feijao's body, I can either launch an attack from the cross-face and hip block position or secure an underhook and execute an attack from the underhook control position.

SECURING UNDERHOOK CONTROL (OPTION 1)

As I have mentioned, creating space and turning on your side gives you a couple of options from the bottom half-guard position. You can execute an attack from the cross-face and hip block position, which I will cover later in the book, or you can work to secure an underhook. The latter is often harder than it sounds. Your opponent's goal from the top half-guard position is to keep your shoulders pinned to the mat and either pepper you with strikes or pass your guard into a more dominant position such as side control or mount, and the easiest way for him to achieve both is to maintain a far-side underhook. If you steal it away from him, expect him to fight tooth and nail to get it back. For this reason, you must transition through the steps quickly. The instant you get up to your side, immediately secure an underhook and either transition to your opponent's back or reverse your positioning by executing a sweep. I demonstrate how to apply both types of attacks later in this section, but first it is important that you become a master at securing the underhook. It's the gateway to your offense from the half guard.

Feijao is in my half guard, pinning my back to the mat. I've managed to secure the cross-face and hip block position by wedging my left arm underneath his chin and posting my right hand on his left hip. I have several attacks I can utilize from here, but instead I decide to secure an underhook. Since I have his right leg trapped between my legs, my goal is to secure an underhook with my left arm.

To create separation between Feijao's body and mine, I drive my left forearm into his neck and push on his left hip with my right hand. As his weight shifts off of my chest, I turn toward my right side.

Continuing to roll onto my right side, I dive my left hand underneath Feijao's body and right arm.

I hook my left arm underneath Feijao's right arm. Next, I wrap my left arm around his back and secure an underhook.

To create even more separation between our bodies, I drive my left arm into the right side of Feijao's body and sit up.

I post my right elbow on the mat.

I step my left leg over Feijao's right leg to prevent him from passing my guard.

To secure the underhook control position, I plant my left foot on the mat between Feijao's legs. It is important to notice that I have positioned my head underneath his head. This prevents him from driving his weight back into me and once again pinning my back to the mat. From here, I will immediately begin my attack by either transitioning to his back or executing a sweep.

HALF GUARD BASICS

SECURING UNDERHOOK CONTROL (OPTION 2)

As you now know, getting up to your side and establishing an underhook allows you to get offensive from the bottom half-guard position. In the previous sequence I demonstrated how to obtain an underhook when your opponent pins your back to the mat. It's an excellent technique to use when in that terrible position, but establishing an underhook is much easier before your opponent has a chance to flatten you out. If your opponent is postured up when he falls in your half guard or he postures up while in your half guard to strike, employing the technique demonstrated below is a phenomenal option. By positioning a knee in front of his shoulder, you not only hinder him from striking, but you also free up one of your arms. When you use that arm to land a few hard punches to your opponent's face, it makes securing the underhook all that much easier.

Feijao is postured up in my half guard. To maintain separation between our bodies, I've placed my left foot on his right hip and positioned my left knee in front of his right shoulder. To control his arms, I'm gripping the back of his right triceps with my left hand and the back of his left triceps with my right hand.

Releasing my left grip on Feijao's arm, I draw my hand back to throw a hook to his jaw.

I land a left hook to Feijao's jaw.

I pull my left hand behind my head.

I throw my left arm straight down and land a hammer fist to the left side of Feijao's face. To guarantee that I cause damage and distract him with the blow, I connect using the outside of my wrist. After all, the boney part of your arm is much harder than padded gloves.

With Feijao stunned from my strikes, I kick my left leg toward the mat and use that momentum to help me sit up. As my back comes off the mat, I dive my left arm underneath his right arm.

To secure underhook control, I wrap my left arm around Feijao's back, plant my right elbow on the mat, and grab his left wrist with my right hand. From here, I will immediately attack by transitioning to his back, which I demonstrate how to do in the following sequence.

KNEE CRANK TO BACK TRANSITION

In the sequence below I demonstrate how to transition to your opponent's back when you establish underhook control from the bottom half-guard position. The first step in this technique is to use your feet to apply a nasty crank on your opponent's trapped leg. When done properly, it becomes extremely difficult for him to clamp down on your underhook with a tight whizzer and flatten your back to the mat by driving into you. This allows you to make a quick and smooth transition to his back. However, if your opponent manages to establish a tight whizzer on your underhook arm before you can apply the crank on his leg, it can be difficult to pull this technique off. In such a situation, you'll want to utilize one of the other techniques in this section.

1

Feijao is in my half guard. Having established underhook control, I will immediately begin my attack.

2

To prevent Feijao from passing my guard, I step my left foot over his trapped right leg.

I slide my right foot out from between Feijao's legs and then hook it around the outside of his right knee.

I curl my left heel toward my buttocks, pulling the lower portion of Feijao's right leg toward me. At the same time, I push his right knee toward his opposite leg using my right foot. The combination of these two actions cranks on his right leg and weakens his base. To capitalize, I drive my left underhook into his right side and chuck his weight forward, forcing him to plant his right hand on the mat. Notice how I can now pull my head out from underneath his right arm.

Still applying the crank on Feijao's right leg, I wrap my left hand around his left side, pull his body into me, get up onto my right knee, and pull my head out from underneath his posted right arm.

I clear my entire head out from underneath Feijao's right arm, post my right hand on the mat, and position my chest over his back.

The instant I climb onto Feijao's back, I cock my right arm back to throw a punch. It's important to note that I'm keeping his hips pinned to my body using my left hand. This prevents him from rolling over his left shoulder and escaping to his guard.

I throw a right uppercut underneath Feijao's right arm and strike his chin. From here, I can continue to strike or work on establishing my second hook and securing the back position.

DUCK UNDER TO BACK TRANSITION

The duck under to back transition is another excellent technique that you can utilize when you've secured underhook control from the bottom half-guard position. The first step is to escape your leg out from underneath your opponent and plant your knee on the mat off to his side. His most common reaction will be to cinch down on your underhook with a tight whizzer, throw his weight forward into your near shoulder, and try to break you back down to the mat. To use his forward energy against him, twist your body and duck underneath his whizzer. Having eliminated his overhook, his forward momentum will cause him to fall face-first into the mat, allowing you to spin around behind him and take his back. To be successful with this technique, it is imperative that you execute all steps in one fluid motion. If you hesitate, your opponent will be able to adjust his position and counter your transition.

Feijao is in my half guard and I've secured the underhook control position. Notice how I have placed my head underneath his chin to prevent him from driving his weight into me and flattening my back to the mat.

I immediately begin my attack by posting my right hand on the mat and driving my left arm into Feijao's right side. Notice how he has wrapped his right arm around my left arm, securing an overhook, or whizzer.

Still driving my left arm into Feijao's right side, I lift my hips off the mat and slide my right leg out from underneath his body.

I pull my right leg underneath me and then plant my knee on the mat.

I step my left leg to the outside of Feijao's right leg, plant my left foot on the mat between our bodies, and drop down to my right elbow. Notice how I have positioned my body at roughly a ninety degree angle in relation to my opponent's body. This creates space between us, which will allow me to drop underneath his right arm and eliminate the whizzer he has on my left arm. If you fail to acquire this angle, the transition will be difficult to manage.

6

I wrap my left arm around the back of Feijao's right arm, and then drive my weight into the back of his arm. In addition to preventing him from posturing up, it also prevents him from turning away from me and pulling guard. At the same time, I duck my head underneath his right arm and begin sliding my right leg underneath my left leg.

7

I slide my right leg underneath my left leg and escape my head out from underneath Feijao's right arm.

8

Having slipped underneath Feijao's right arm, his forward momentum carries his face toward the mat. To capitalize on his positioning, I drive off the mat using my left foot and reach my left arm over his back.

As I hook my left arm around Feijao's left side, I climb up to my knees and circle around behind him to take his back.

I slide my left knee underneath Feijao's right hip, post my right foot on the mat, and then cock my right arm back to begin a ground and pound assault.

UNDERHOOK CONTROL

I throw a right uppercut underneath Feijao's right arm and strike him in the chin.

I cock my right hand back to land another punch.

To avoid getting struck with another uppercut, Feijao lifts his head up. The instant he does this, I throw a right hook over the top of his right arm and strike the side of his face.

UNDERHOOK REVERSE SWEEP

The underhook reverse sweep is another technique that involves forcing a reaction out of your opponent and then using that reaction to transition to a dominant position. The first step is to drive your underhook into your opponent's side as though you were trying to drive him over to his side. The majority of the time, this will cause him to counter by establishing a tight overhook and driving his weight into your near shoulder. Instead of resisting that energy, you go with it by falling to your side, underhooking his far leg, and then using his inward pressure to drive him over to his back. As with all the half-guard techniques I demonstrate, fluidity of movement is mandatory for success. The instant your opponent drives his weight into your shoulder, you want to underhook his leg and power him over. If you hesitate, he will stop his forward momentum and prevent you from executing the sweep.

Feijao is in my half guard and I've secured the underhook control position. Notice how I have placed my head underneath his chin to prevent him from driving his weight into me and flattening my back to the mat.

I post my right hand on the mat and drive my left arm into Feijao's right side. At the same time, I elevate my hips off the mat and begin pulling my right leg out from underneath his body. Feijao has wrapped his right arm around my left arm, securing an overhook, or whizzer.

UNDERHOOK CONTROL

Keeping my hips elevated by driving off the mat with my left foot and right arm, I pull my right leg out from underneath Feijao's body and post my knee on the mat. Immediately Feijao counters by tightening his overhook around my left arm and driving his weight forward. Instead of resisting his energy, I will use it to my advantage by sweeping him to his back.

As Feijao drives his weight into me, I fall to my right hip and elbow. Notice how this causes him to lurch forward.

Dropping down to my right side, I wrap my right arm around Feijao's left leg and begin rolling toward my left.

While Feijao's energy is still moving forward, I roll over my left shoulder and use my right underhook on his left leg to power him over toward his back. Notice that I have my right leg hooked around the back of his right leg to prevent him from posting his foot on the mat and blocking the sweep.

Having been fluid with my movements, Feijao gets swept to his back.

I follow Feijao over and land on top in his half guard. From here, I will immediately work to pass his half guard and move into side control.

WHIZZER TRAP UNDERHOOK REVERSE SWEEP

In the previous move you drove your underhook into your opponent's side, causing him to counter by establishing a tight overhook and driving his weight back into you. In this scenario, there is no need to bait your opponent into such a reaction—he establishes a tight overhook and drives his weight forward the instant you secure underhook control. Just as with the underhook reverse sweep, you establish an underhook on his far leg and use his forward pressure to power him over to his back, but because you're on your side rather than your knees, the technique requires more finesse. To be successful, you must trap your opponent's whizzer arm to his body as you execute the sweep—something that wasn't necessary with the underhook reverse sweep due to the speed and force of the technique. If you fail to do this, your opponent will be able to post his hand on the mat and block the sweep.

Feijao is in my half guard and I've secured the underhook control position. Notice how I have placed my head underneath his chin to prevent him from driving his weight into me and flattening my back to the mat.

In an attempt to pin my back to the mat, Feijao cinches down on my left underhook with a tight whizzer and drives his weight into me. The instant I feel this pressure, I release my underhook and grab his right wrist with my left hand.

    MASTERING MIXED MARTIAL ARTS

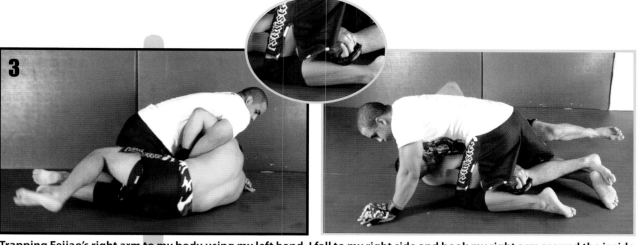

3

Trapping Feijao's right arm to my body using my left hand, I fall to my right side and hook my right arm around the inside of his left leg.

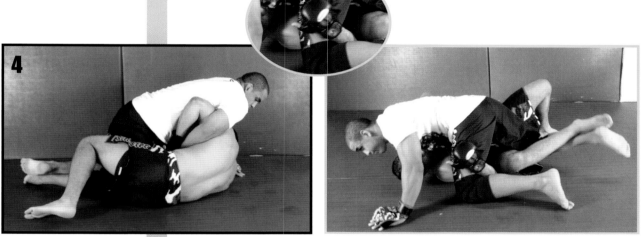

4

I hook my right arm around the back of Feijao's left leg.

5

While Feijao is still driving his weight forward, I roll toward my left side and lift his left leg off the mat using my right arm. Notice how I have my right leg hooked around the back of his right leg to prevent him from posting his foot on the mat and blocking the sweep.

Rolling over my left shoulder, I power Feijao toward his back using my right underhook. Notice that I'm still controlling his right arm with my left hand to prevent him from posting his hand on the mat and blocking the sweep.

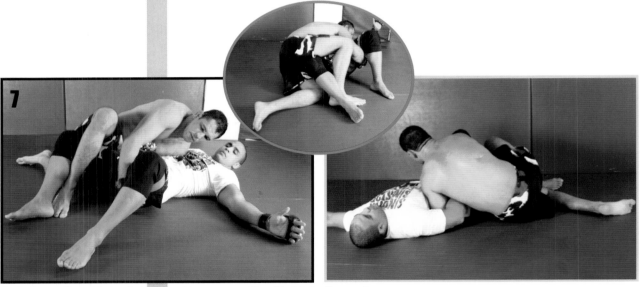

As Feijao rolls to his back, I follow him over and land in his half guard.

Before Feijao can lock his legs together and trap me in his half guard, I transition to side control by stepping my right leg toward the outside of his right leg.

As I turn my chest toward Feijao's chest, I position my right leg to the outside of his right leg.

I post my right knee on the mat next to Feijao's right hip, sprawl my left leg back, and collapse my chest over his torso.

I sweep my left hand across the mat toward Feijao's head, breaking his overhook on my left arm. Once accomplished, I release my underhook on Feijao's left leg an begin working to secure a right underhook on his left arm. It is important to note that if you release your opponent's leg before you break his overhook on your arm, he will be able to force a scramble and prevent you from securing the side control position.

I slide my left knee underneath Feijao's right shoulder, sprawl my right leg back, and drop my weight over his torso. At the same time, I wrap my right arm underneath his left arm, wrap my left arm around the back of his head, and grip my hands together above his left shoulder.

To secure side control, I slide my right knee up to Feijao's right hip and distribute my weight over his chest.

ARM DRAG TO BACK TRANSITION

The majority of the time your opponent will counter the first technique you throw at him. For this reason, it is vital that you string your attacks together based upon his reactions. In the sequence below, I attempt to sweep my opponent using the whizzer trap reverse sweep from underhook control, but he counters by sprawling his leg back. Instead of giving up and allowing him to pin my back to the mat, I use his reaction to execute the arm drag to back transition. If he had blocked this attack, I would have move on to another. It doesn't matter if your opponent blocks ten attacks in a row—as long as you keep them coming, you'll eventually get one step ahead of him and be successful.

At the end of this sequence, you end up in the back position with an inside hook on your opponent's leg. This gives you several options. You can flatten him out on the mat and employ ground and pound (sequence A), you can establish your second hook and secure control of the back position (sequence B), or you can work for a ten-finger guillotine choke (sequence C). Learning all three options allows you to capitalize on a particular opponent's weaknesses. If he has terrible ground and pound defense, flattening him out and employing strikes will produce positive results. If he is a master and protecting himself from strikes but has horrible submission defense, then employing the guillotine choke or securing your second hook and applying a rear choke will produce positive results. The important thing is that you always remain on the offense. If there are lulls in your attacks, your opponent will have a better chance at finding a hole to escape.

Feijao is in my half guard and I've secured the underhook control position. Notice how I have placed my head underneath his chin to prevent him from driving his weight into me and flattening my back to the mat.

UNDERHOOK CONTROL

In an attempt to pin my back to the mat, Feijao tightens down on my left arm with his overhook and drives his weight into me. The instant I feel this pressure I release my underhook and grab his right wrist with my left hand.

Using my left hand to trap Feijao's right arm to my body, I drop down to my right side to execute the whizzer trap reverse sweep. Sensing the sweep coming, Feijao counters by sprawling his left leg back and dropping his hips to the mat. With his weight now spread out, it will be impossible for me to hook his leg and power him over to his back using the underhook reversal. Instead of forcing a technique that won't work, I will immediately transition to the arm drag.

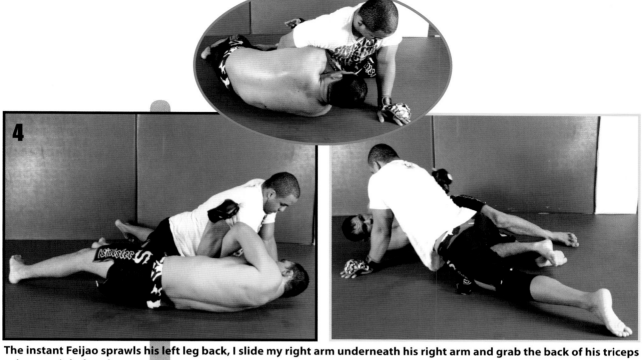

4

The instant Feijao sprawls his left leg back, I slide my right arm underneath his right arm and grab the back of his triceps using my right hand.

5

Having established the arm drag position, I pull Feijao's right arm toward the right side of my body using my right grip and begin sitting up.

6 Still pulling Feijao's right arm toward my right side, I sit up, twist my body in a clockwise direction, and reach my left arm over his back.

7 Having been fluid with my movements, Feijao falls forward and posts his right hand on the mat. To capitalize on his positioning, I post my right hand on the mat and grab his left hip using my left hand. Next, I use my grip on his waist to pull his body into me. Not only does this prevent him from rolling and establishing the guard position, but it will also help me secure control of his back.

Using my left grip on Feijao's waist as an anchor, I climb up to my right knee and cock my right hand back to throw strikes. Notice that my right leg is still hooked around the inside of Feijao's right leg.

I throw a right hook to the right side of Feijao's face.

SINGLE HOOK CONTROL **SEQUENCE A: FLATTENING OPPONENT**

When you utilize one of the techniques in the book to transition from guard or half guard to your opponent's back, you'll usually have one hook established on his legs. As I have mentioned, this gives you several options: You can work to establish your second hook and secure the position, apply a guillotine choke, or flatten his body to the mat using your single hook, which is the technique demonstrated below. If you look at the photos, you'll notice that I begin the technique by wedging my arm to the inside of my opponent's far leg. This acts as my second hook, and better allows me to flatten my opponent out. As you can see, once he's belly down, it becomes very difficult for him to defend against my punches. To learn how to employ your other options from single hook control, see the following sequences.

I have managed to transition from the half guard to Feijao's back. Notice how my right leg is hooked around the inside of his right leg. From this position, I have several options. In this particular case I decide to flatten my opponent out with my single hook and employ ground and pound.

I ball my left hand into a fist.

I punch my left fist to the inside of Feijao's left leg.

I wedge my left arm to the inside of Feijao's left leg to serve as my second hook. It is important to mention that the knuckles of my left hand are flush against the inside of his left thigh.

I pull my right leg toward my right side and straighten my left arm into Feijao's left leg. The combination of these actions stretches his legs apart and flattens his body to the mat. The moment I establish this control, I cock my right arm back and prepare to unleash a ground and pound assault.

6

I land a right hook to the right side of
Feijao's head.

SINGLE HOOK CONTROL **SEQUENCE B: SECURING CONTROL OF THE BACK**

My goal in this sequence is the same as in the last—to flatten my opponent out on the mat. However, instead of accomplishing this task from single hook control, I first establish my second hook and secure the back position. Once I've forced my opponent's stomach to the mat using both hooks, I can punch the sides of his head, apply a rear choke, or do a combination of both. To see how the rear choke is performed in detail, revisit the open guard section.

1

I have managed to transition from the half guard to Feijao's back. Notice how my right leg is hooked around the inside of his right leg. From this position, I have several options. In this particular case I decide to establish my second hook to secure the back position, flatten my opponent out, land some strikes, and then work for a rear choke.

2

I dive my left hand underneath Feijao's left arm.

3

I grab the top of Feijao's left wrist with my left hand and then pull his arm into his body.

4

Having created the space I need to establish my second hook, I throw my left leg over Feijao's back.

5

I hook my left foot to the inside of Feijao's left leg.

I hook my left foot deeper around the inside of Feijao's left leg. Next, I flatten his chest to the mat by sprawling my legs back and driving my hips into his lower back.

Having broken Feijao down to the mat, I cock my right arm back.

I punch Feijao in the right side of his jaw. From here, I can continue throwing strikes or work to secure the rear choke.

SINGLE HOOK CONTROL SEQUENCE C: TEN-FINGER GUILLOTINE CHOKE

Applying the ten-finger guillotine choke is another option when you take your opponent's back and have single hook control. Unlike the traditional guillotine choke, it cuts off blood to your opponent's brain rather than just air, forcing him to either quickly tap or pass out. The only downside to the technique is that if you fail to finish your opponent with the submission, you'll be stuck in the bottom half-guard position. Due to this negative aspect, it is important to weigh your options. If you have any doubt about your ability to properly lock in the choke, you'll probably want to utilize the previous technique to secure the back position, flatten your opponent out, and apply a rear choke. To better illustrate how to properly apply the ten-finger grip used in this guillotine variation, I've provided an alternate view in sequence C1.

1

I have managed to transition from the half guard to Feijao's back. Notice how my right leg is hooked around the inside of his right leg. From this position, I have several options. In this particular case I decide to transition to the guillotine choke. To begin, I cock my right arm back.

2

I throw a right hook to the right side of Feijao's jaw.

Instead of pulling my right arm back to land more punches, I reach my right hand around the left side of his head.

I wrap my right arm around the left side of Feijao's head.

I grab Feijao's right triceps with my right hand, twist my body in a counterclockwise direction, and drop toward my right hip.

SINGLE HOOK CONTROL

6

Continuing to twist my body in a counterclockwise direction, I form a ten-finger grip with my hands and roll toward my back. Notice how Feijao's right arm is now trapped between our bodies.

7

Staying on my right side, I roll toward my back.

8

To prevent Feijao from rolling forward and escaping the choke, I throw my left leg over his back and apply downward pressure. To prevent him from passing my guard, I keep my right leg hooked around the inside of his right leg. To finish the guillotine choke, I pinch my elbows to my body and squeeze everything tight. With my right arm cutting into the left side of his neck and his right shoulder cutting into the right side of his neck, I sever the blood flow to his brain. If he doesn't quickly tap, he will go to sleep.

SEQUENCE C1: TEN-FINGER GUILLOTINE GRIP

In this sequence I show in detail how to form the ten-finger grip for the guillotine choke.

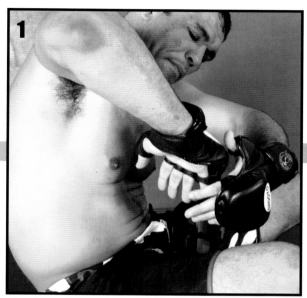

I hook my left index finger around my right pinky finger.

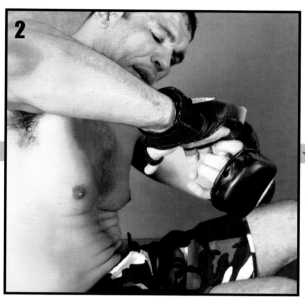

I hook the middle finger of my right hand around the middle finger of my left hand. Next, I hook the ring finger of my right hand around the ring finger of my left hand.

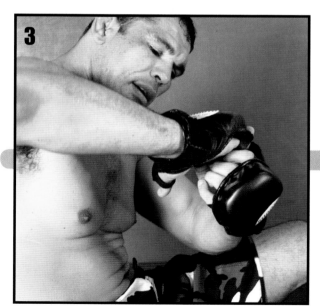

I hook my left pinky around my right index finger.

Now that I've established the ten-finger grip, I pinch my elbows tight to my body and finish the choke.

ARM DRAG TO BACK

By now you should understand the importance of preventing your opponent from flattening your back to the mat when in the bottom half-guard position. I've demonstrated how to use the cross-face and hip block to escape to your side, several ways to establish an underhook, and numerous techniques you can employ from the underhook control position. Now I will take a step back and demonstrate several attacks that you can utilize directly from the cross-face and hip block position. With each of these techniques, the key to success is keeping one arm positioned across your opponent's neck and your opposite hand posted on his far hip. As long as you maintain this control, it will be very difficult for him to drive his weight into you and pin both of your shoulders to the mat. In the sequence below, I demonstrate how to use the cross-face and hip block control position to execute an arm drag and transition to your opponent's back.

Feijao is in my half guard and I've secured the cross-face and hip block position by wedging my left forearm under his chin and driving my right hand into left hip.

To create separation between our bodies, I drive my left arm into Feijao's neck, push on his left hip, scoot my hips toward my left, and turn onto my right side.

Having created space between our bodies with my previous actions, I slide my left shin in front of Feijao's right leg and hip.

To create even more separation, I slide my left knee up Feijao's torso and to the inside of his right arm.

Positioning my left knee in front of Feijao's right shoulder, I roll toward my left shoulder and grab his right wrist with my left hand. Uncomfortable with my new position, Feijao drives his weight forward. To use his energy to my advantage, I will immediately transition to the arm drag. It is important to note that if he were to react to this new position by posturing up, I would not utilize this technique. Instead, I would sit up with him and secure an underhook. To see how this is done, revisit the underhook section of the book.

To capitalize on Feijao's forward energy, I kick my left leg toward the mat and quickly sit up before he can close off the space between us. At the same time, I push his right hand toward my right side using my left hand, dive my right arm underneath his right arm, and grip his right triceps with my right hand.

As I sit all the way up, I pull Feijao's right arm toward my right side using both of my grips.

With Feijao's body still pressing forward, I release my left grip on his right wrist, pull his arm toward my right side using my right grip, and twist my body in a clockwise direction. Fluid with my movements, the combination of these actions causes Feijao to fall forward and post his right hand on the mat.

I reach my left arm over Feijao's back and grab the left side of his waist just above his hip. I then use this grip to pull his body into me, which prevents him from rolling to his back and escaping to guard.

I post my right hand on the mat.

Using my left grip as an anchor, I pull myself up to my right knee and climb onto Feijao's back. Notice how my right leg is still hooked around the inside of his right leg. From here, I have several attack options. I can utilize ground and pound, work for a guillotine choke from the single hook position, or establish my second hook and apply a rear choke. To see how to perform these options, revisit the previous techniques.

ELEVATOR TO BACK TRANSITION

As you now know, your opponent's most common reaction when you secure the cross-face and hip block position will be to drive his weight forward in an attempt to pin your back to the mat. In the previous sequence, you capitalized on this reaction by executing an arm drag and then transitioning to his back. In the sequence below, you again capitalize on his forward pressure by taking his back, but you do so in a different manner. The first step is to establish an inside hook on your opponent's free leg. Next, you use that control along with your arms to lift his body up and throw his weight over the top of you. As his body shoots forward, you slip out from underneath him and take his back. Just like in the previous move, correct timing is essential. If your opponent senses the technique coming and halts his forward energy, the move will be extremely difficult to pull off.

Feijao is in my half guard, and I've secured the cross face and hip block position by wedging my left forearm under his chin and positioning my right hand on his left hip.

To create separation between our bodies, I drive my left arm into Feijao's neck, push on his left hip, scoot my hips toward my left, and turn onto my right side.

I hook my left foot around the inside of Feijao's right knee.

Using Feijao's forward energy to my advantage, I roll to my back, lift his right leg off the mat using my left hook, and elevate his upper body using my arms

5

In one explosive movement, I roll to my left shoulder and throw Feijao's upper body over my head using my arms. It is important to note that I'm using his forward pressure to help rock his upper body over my head. This will create enough space between our bodies for me to slip out from underneath him and take his back.

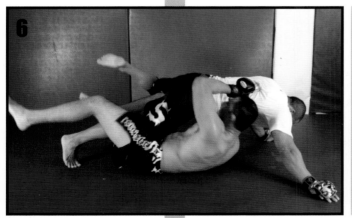

6

As Feijao's upper body shoots over my head, I unhook my left foot from his right leg, kick my left leg toward the mat, and escape my body to my left side.

After escaping my body out from underneath Feijao, I turn onto my right side, post on my right elbow, reach my left arm over the back of his hips, and hook my left hand around the inside of his left thigh.

Using my left grip on Feijao's left leg as an anchor, I pull myself up onto his back, slide my right leg out from underneath his right leg, climb up to my knees, and slide my left shin over the back of his right leg.

CROSS-FACE AND HIP BLOCK POSITION

Keeping my left shin pinned to Feijao's right leg and my left arm wrapped tightly around his waist, I post on my right foot and cock my right arm back.

I land a right hook to the right side of Feijao's head.

I cock my right hand back to throw another punch to Feijao's head.

ANKLE PICK LEVER SWEEP

Sometimes when you secure the cross-face and hip block position, your opponent will reposition his body diagonally across your torso and drive his weight down into your cross-face arm. While it's still possible to maintain space between your bodies using your cross-face, getting up to your side can prove difficult. Instead of fighting your opponent's downward energy in such a scenario, use it against him by employing the ankle pick lever sweep. When done correctly, you'll put him on his back and obtain side control.

Feijao is in my half guard, and I've secured the cross-face and hip block position by wedging my left arm under his chin and posting my right hand on his left hip. To create separation between our bodies, I drive my left arm into his neck and push on his left hip with my right hand.

Feijao distributes his weight over my left arm, which could make getting up to my side difficult to manage. To use his energy against him, I begin transitioning into the ankle pick to lever sweep by rolling toward my left side, guiding his upper body toward my left using my left arm, and establishing an underhook by wrapping my right arm around the inside of his left leg.

I lift my feet toward the ceiling and rock toward my left side. Notice how this action pulls Feijao's right leg toward my left. To maintain his balance, he shifts his weight onto his left leg.

Having repositioned Feijao's right leg to my left side and rocked his weight over my body, I turn onto my left side and reach my left hand toward his right foot.

I grab Feijao's right shin with my left hand, wrap my left leg over his right knee, and then hook my left foot underneath my right leg.

6

Keeping my right arm wrapped tightly around Feijao's left leg, I pull his right foot toward me and extend my left leg into his right leg. The combination of these actions creates a torque on his right leg. Unable to post his left leg behind him due to my right underhook, he begins to fall backward.

7

As I continue to pull on Feijao's right shin with my left hand and extend my left leg into his right leg, I rock my weight toward my right side, sit up, and begin sliding my right leg out from underneath his right leg.

8

As Feijao falls to his back, I turn onto my right side and continue to slide my right leg out from underneath his right leg.

I release my grip on Feijao's right leg and climb up to my knees.

I post my left knee on the mat, sprawl my right leg back, drop my weight down on Feijao's torso, wrap my left arm around the back of his head, and drive my left shoulder into the right side of his jaw.

In order to pass Feijao's half guard, I need to free my right leg. To begin this process, I rotate my hips into his right leg.

Having broken Feijao's hook on my right leg, I curl my heel toward my right buttock.

I pull my right leg out from between Feijao's legs.

I step my right leg over my left leg.

I scissor my legs and slide my right knee up to Feijao's right hip. To secure side control, I wrap my right arm underneath his left arm, grip my hands together behind his left shoulder, and drop my weight down on his torso to pin his shoulders to the mat.

HALF GUARD TO TRIANGLE

When in the bottom half guard position, the majority of the time I will either sweep my opponent or transition to his back. Of the handful of submissions that I will employ from the position, the triangle is at the top of the list. To set it up, you must get onto your side and secure an overhook. This can be very difficult to manage when your opponent is pinning your back to the mat and driving his weight forward, so this technique is best utilized once you've created space and established the cross-face and hip block position. Although it might seem like a difficult move to pull off, after a few repetitions in the gym, you'll be submitting your opponents with it in no time. I strongly suggest learning this move because it is a very sneaky technique that will often catch your opponent off guard.

Feijao is in my half guard. Having created space between our bodies using the cross-face and hip block position, I secure a left overhook on his right arm and grab his left wrist with my right hand.

I drive my left arm into the back of Feijao's right shoulder and shrimp my hips toward my left side.

Having created space between our bodies, I slide my left shin across the front of Feijao's hips.

I drive my left shin into Feijao's hips, causing him to lurch forward. At the same time, I force his left arm to the inside of his left leg using my right hand and slide my right leg out from between his legs. It is important to mention that I'm still cinching down on his right arm with a tight left overhook. If your overhook is weak, your opponent can nullify your attack by posturing up.

As I escape my right leg out from underneath Feijao's body, I release my grip on his left wrist, roll toward my left shoulder, and throw my right leg over his left arm. It's important to mention that I'm driving my left shin into his hips to maintain distance and keep his upper body collapsed forward.

I wrap my right leg around the left side of Feijao's head.

I hook my right foot underneath my left leg.

I grab Feijao's right arm with both of my hands, elevate my hips off the mat, and then force his arm toward the right side of my body.

I pin Feijao's right arm to my right leg using both of my hands. Next, I drop my hips to the mat, trapping his right arm across his face.

Keeping Feijao's right arm pinned to my hip using my right hand, I place my left foot on his right hip and grab my right instep with my left hand. Next, I push off his right hip with my left foot, escape my hips toward my left side, and pull my right leg over the back of his neck.

I throw my left leg over my right foot. Next, I curl my left leg downward into my right foot, which in turn drives my right leg into the back of Feijao's head. Squeezing everything tight, his right arm drives into the right side of his neck and my right leg drives into the left side of his neck, forcing him to tap. It is important to notice that I've maintained my left grip on my right leg. This helps prevent Feijao from posturing up and escaping the submission.

BRIDGE SWEEP

Sometimes an opponent in your half guard will pin his chest to your chest, establish an over-under body lock, and drive his weight forward to pin your shoulders to the mat. When under this type of dominating control, it can be difficult to wedge your hand underneath his neck and apply a cross-face to create separation. Although it might seem like an impossible position from which to be offensive, there are a few techniques that you can employ to reverse the position. The first technique I'll attempt is the bridge sweep, a simple and effective maneuver that works a large percentage of the time. The best part about the bridge sweep is that if your opponent defends against it by counterbalancing his weight, you can use his defense to your advantage by transitioning to the bridge to reverse sweep, which I demonstrate in the next sequence. If the bridge to reverse sweep fails, all is not lost. The chances are you'll have created enough space between your bodies with the two techniques to establish underhook control or the cross-face and hip block position. The most important thing is not to stall when you find yourself dominated in this fashion. If you hesitate to employ the bridge sweep, your opponent will have an opportunity to pass your guard into a superior position such as side control.

Feijao is in my half guard, pinning my shoulders to the mat with an over-under body lock. I have already tried to establish a cross face, but his hold is too tight.

I drive my right fist into Feijao's left hip. At the same time, I push his right shoulder toward our legs using my left hand. My goal with these two actions is to bait him into throwing his body forward, which will allow me to use his momentum to sweep him to his back.

Feijao counters my pressure by throwing his weight forward and digging his left shoulder into my face. The instant he does this, I flare my arms out to my sides.

I sweep my left arm into the right side of Feijao's face and chop my right arm into his left knee.

5

Continuing with my previous actions, I unhook my right leg from Feijao's right leg, drive off the mat using my left foot, and roll over my right shoulder. With Feijao still driving his weight forward, my actions force him to barrel roll over his left shoulder.

6

I continue to roll over my right shoulder.

7

Having been explosive with my movements, Feijao is forced over to his back.

8

As Feijao rolls to his back, I follow him over and land in his half guard.

BRIDGE TO REVERSE SWEEP

Although the bridge sweep is highly effective, it's not uncommon for your opponent to block it by counterbalancing his weight. For example, if you have your opponent's right leg trapped and you attempt to sweep him toward your right using the bridge sweep, he can counter by driving his weight forward and toward your left side. To counter his counter, immediately sweep him to your left side using the bridge to reverse sweep. With his weight already distributed to your left side, the technique is extremely effective. However, in order for it to work, you must have exceptional timing and employ explosive movements. The goal is to execute the reverse sweep while your opponent is still shifting his weight to counter the bridge sweep, and the only way to do this is to develop nail-sharp timing and employ explosive movements.

Feijao is in my half guard, pinning my shoulders to the mat with an over-under body lock. I have already tried to establish a cross-face, but his hold is too tight.

I attempt to reverse Feijao with the bridge sweep by driving my left arm into the right side of his face and chopping my right arm into his left knee.

3

Continuing with my previous actions, I attempt to roll over my right shoulder.

4

Feijao counters the bridge sweep by driving his weight toward my left side. To use his defense to my advantage, I imme-diately begin transitioning into the bridge to reverse sweep by wrapping my left arm around his right arm. As long as I maintain this overhook, he won't be able to block the sweep by posting his hand on the mat.

5

As Feijao redistributes his weight to my left side to counter the bridge sweep, I drive my right fist into his left hip, wrap my left leg over the back of his right leg to prevent him from posting his foot on the mat and blocking the sweep, and roll toward my left.

6

I roll over my left shoulder and power Feijao over using my right arm. Having trapped his right arm and right leg, he is unable to counter the sweep.

7

I sweep Feijao over to his back.

8

I slide my left leg out from underneath Feijao's right leg and then drive my left knee into his right hip. At the same time, I rotate my chest toward his chest.

9

I grab Feijao's right triceps with my left hand and begin sliding my left leg underneath my right leg.

Pulling up on Feijao's right triceps using my left hand, I pull my left leg out from underneath my right leg, post my left foot on the mat, slide my right arm underneath his left arm, and drop my weight down on his torso.

To secure side control, I slide my left foot toward Feijao's head, pull his right arm off the mat using my left hand, and drop my right hip to the mat. With his shoulders pinned, I can now execute an attack.

COUNTERING THE PASS

There are countless ways for an opponent to pass your half guard into the side control position, but in the sequence below my opponent employs one of the more common methods. Wrapping his arms around my legs and hugging them tight, he sprawls his trapped leg back to free it from my control, circles around to the outside of my legs, and then moves into side control. However, he has only won half the battle. In order to complete the transition, he must first secure the side control position. In this sequence, he attempts to do so by turning his back toward my head and reaching his near arm over my body. If I allow him to accomplish his goal, all his weight will come crashing down on my chest, pinning my back to the mat. To prevent this from happening, I sit up into him the as he reaches his arm over my body. This creates a good deal of space between us, allowing me to escape my hips out from underneath him, circle around behind him, and take his back.

In an attempt to pass my half guard, Feijao has wrapped his arms around my legs and hugged them tight to his body. With my legs pinched together, it is difficult for me to keep him trapped in my half guard.

Feijao sprawls his right leg back, breaking my control.

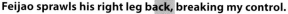

Feijao circles around to the outside of my right leg.

As Feijao passes my guard, I begin sitting up and turning toward my right side.

In an attempt to pin my back to the mat, Feijao moves his left arm over my torso. His goal is to position his left arm on the left side of my body, throw his right leg over his left leg, turn his back toward my head, and pin my shoulders to the mat by distributing his weight over my chest. To prevent him from accomplishing this, I continue to sit up and turn toward my right side.

Taking advantage of the opening created by Feijao's transition, I sit all the way up, post my right hand on the mat, and wrap my left arm over his back.

Posting on my right hand and left foot, I pull my right leg out from underneath my body.

Having created space with my previous actions, I twist my body in a counterclockwise direction, hook my right foot to the inside of Feijao's left leg, and escape my hips out from underneath his body.

Coming down onto my left buttock, I drive my right foot into Feijao's left leg. With my body no longer underneath him, he falls face first to the mat.

Still rotating my body in a counterclockwise direction, I post my left hand on the mat and wrap my right arm over Feijao's back. Once accomplished, I pull him into me using my right hand. This anchor will not only help me climb up onto his back, but it also prevents him from rolling over his right shoulder and escaping to guard.

I unhook my right foot from the inside of Feijao's right leg and then sprawl my right leg back. At the same time, I begin lifting my hips off the mat.

As I circle around to Feijao's back, I hook my left foot around the inside of his left leg.

Having secured an inside hook, I cock my left arm back and prepare to throw strikes. It is important to mention that I'm still pulling on Feijao's right side using my right hand. This keeps his hips pinned to my hips and prevents him from rolling forward and pulling me into his guard. From here, I have several options: I can stay in this position, flatten his belly to the mat, and implement some ground and pound; I can secure my second hook and work my attacks from the back position; or I can transition to a guillotine choke. To see these options, revisit the previous section.

The downed guard is when you're lying on your back and your opponent is hovering above you in the standing position. There are many ways to end up in this position, the most common being your opponent simply climbs to his feet while in your guard. In this portion of the section, I demonstrate a couple of methods for combating this situation. If your opponent is close, I show how to drop him to his back by executing a sweep. If he maintains distance, I demonstrate a technique for escaping back to your feet. In addition to this, I also show several ways to control your opponent's distance to prevent him from closing the gap and landing hard punches. If you find yourself in this type of scenario and are unsure what to do, your opponent can cause some serious damage. For this reason, I strongly suggest spending an ample amount of time perfecting the techniques offered.

INSIDE HOOK PUSH SWEEP

There are several ways that you can end up on your back with your opponent standing above you. The most common scenario is for him to posture up in your guard and then quickly climb to his feet. Once he's up, he has all sorts of options at his disposal, such as kicking your legs, dropping punches to your body and head, or throwing your legs to the side to pass your guard. To prevent him from employing these options, immediately put him on his back using the inside hook push sweep. The goal is to execute the sweep before he can establish a solid base on his feet. If you fail to do this and he backs out of your guard to create space, you'll want to use one of the other techniques demonstrated in this section.

Feijao is postured up in my closed guard with his hands on my hips.

Feijao posts his right foot on the mat.

As Feijao stands up in my guard, I unhook my feet and grab his right ankle with my left hand.

As Feijao postures, I place my left foot on his right hip.

I drive my left foot into Feijao's right hip. To maintain his balance, he steps his left foot back. The instant he does this, I shoot my right foot between his legs. It is important to notice that I'm cupping my hand around his heel—this prevents him from escaping his foot as I work to sweep him to his back.

I hook my right foot around the back of Feijao's left knee.

I pull Feijao's right heel toward me using my left hand. At the same time, I drive my left foot into his right hip to push him backward and pull my right foot toward me to collapse his left knee.

The combination of my actions forces Feijao to fall to his back. As he goes down, I rock my body forward and sit up. Notice that I have maintained control of his right foot using my left hand. This prevents him from escaping to his feet as I work to the standing position.

Elevating Feijao's right leg off the mat using my left hand, I post on my right hand and left foot and begin sliding my right leg underneath my body.

I slide my right leg out from underneath my body and post my right knee on the mat.

Still controlling Feijao's right foot with my left hand, I stand up.

Rotating my hips in a clockwise direction, I throw Feijao's right leg toward my right side and cock my right hand back. Notice how my rotation has spring-loaded my hips for an overhand right.

Having cleared Feijao's legs out of the way, I rotate my body in a counterclockwise direction, shift a larger portion of my weight onto my left leg, and throw an overhand right to his face.

SWEEPS

DE LA RIVA SWEEP

When you're lying on your back with your opponent standing above you, utilizing the De La Riva sweep allows you to create space between your bodies. Once accomplished, you can use that space to either climb to your feet or circle around behind him and take his back. With jiu-jitsu being my specialty, I usually opt to take my opponent's back, which I demonstrate how to do in the sequence below.

Feijao is postured up in my closed guard with his hands on my hips.

Feijao posts his right foot on the mat.

As Feijao stands up in my guard, I unhook my feet, draw my right knee toward my chest, and then place my right foot on his left hip. At the same time, I grab his right ankle with my left hand to prevent him from escaping his foot as I execute the sweep.

I drive my right foot into Feijao's abdomen. To maintain his balance, Feijao steps his left foot behind him.

Keeping my hips elevated off the mat, I wrap my left leg around the outside of Feijao's right leg.

Maintaining my grip on Feijao's right ankle, I dive my left leg between his legs and then hook my left foot around the front of his left leg. Next, I straighten my left leg and twist his right ankle in a counterclockwise direction using my left hand. The combination of these actions forces him to rotate in a counterclockwise direction.

I continue to straighten my left leg into Feijao's left leg and twist his ankle in a counterclockwise direction using my left hand. As his body turns in a counterclockwise direction, his back becomes exposed.

I pull Feijao's left leg off the mat using my left hand, causing him to fall face-first to the mat. Immediately I sit up and elevate his right leg off the mat to prevent him from freeing his leg and escaping back to his feet.

Still controlling Feijao's right leg using my left hand, I slide my right leg out from underneath his left leg and climb up to my right knee.

I release my grip on Feijao's right foot and cock my right hand back.

I throw a right hook to the right side of Feijao's face.

SWEEPS

INSIDE HOOK CONTROL TO TRIP SWEEP

When you're lying on your back and your opponent is standing above you with a solid base, he has a lot of mobility. He can move backward to avoid sweep attempts, and he can quickly come forward to land strikes. To stifle his ability to move forward, I'll place my foot on the hip of his rear leg. To hinder him from retreating backward, I'll hook my opposite foot around the inside of his near leg. A lot of times this control will frustrate your opponent, causing him to throw a haymaker with his rear hand in an attempt to clear your control. In such a scenario, you can use your control to not only avoid his strike, but also transition into the trip sweep demonstrated below.

I've secured inside hook control from the downed guard by hooking my right foot to the inside of Feijao's left leg and planting my left foot on his right hip.

Feijao throws an overhand right toward my face. To prevent him from closing the distance and landing his punch, I drive my left foot into his right hip.

Having avoided Feijao's strike, I turn onto my right side and grab the back of his left ankle with my right hand.

I chop my right foot into the back of Feijao's right leg.

Still pushing on Feijao's left hip using my left foot, I kick his right leg out from underneath him and pull his left foot toward my head. The combination of my actions forces him to fall to his back.

As Feijao falls to his back, I immediately rock my body forward and sit up.

Keeping Feijao's left foot elevated using my right hand, I post my left foot on the mat.

I stand up.

Rotating my hips in a counterclockwise direction, I throw Feijao's left leg toward my left side and cock my left hand back. Notice how my rotation has spring-loaded my hips to throw a powerful strike with my left hand.

Having cleared Feijao's legs, I rotate my body in a clockwise direction and throw a powerful left hook to his face.

SWEEPS

TRIP KICK TO SINGLE LEG

In this sequence I demonstrate how to disrupt your opponent's base and balance from the downed guard position by turning onto your side and throwing a round kick at his lead leg. While he works to reestablish his balance, you quickly climb to your knees and transition into the high single position. Once accomplished, you can turn the tide of battle by executing a takedown.

I'm lying on my back with Feijao standing in front of me. To maintain distance, I've placed my right foot on his left knee and my left foot on his right hip.

I position my left foot to the inside of Feijao's right leg, post my left elbow on the mat, and roll onto my left side.

I throw a right round kick to the outside of Feijao's left knee. As the kick lands, I curl my left leg into his left foot. The combination of these actions rotates Feijao's body in a clockwise direction and exposes his back.

Posting my left hand and right foot on the mat, I begin working up to my feet.

Driving forward, I hook my left arm around Feijao's left leg and wrap my right arm around his back. Notice how my head is positioned to the inside of his body rather than the outside.

SWEEPS

6

I wrap my right arm around the back of Feijao's left leg.

7

Standing up, I trap Feijao's left leg between my legs by sliding my left foot next to my right foot. At the same time, I grab my left triceps with my right hand. To secure the high single position, I lift his left leg off the mat using my grips, pin his leg to my chest, and pinch my knees together. From here, I can work to take him to the mat with a single leg takedown.

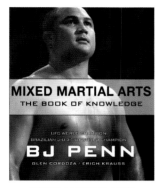

MIXED MARTIAL ARTS

BJ PENN

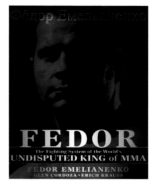

WRESTLING FOR FIGHTING

RANDY COUTURE

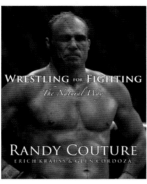

FEDOR

FEDOR
EMELIANENKO

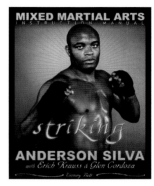

***MIXED MARTIAL ARTS
INSTRUCTION MANUAL***

ANDERSON SILVA

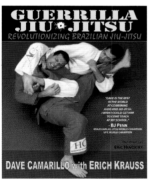

GUERRILLA JIU-JITSU

DAVE CAMARILLO

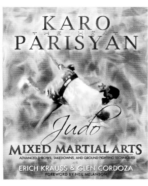

JUDO FOR MIXED MARTIAL ARTS

KARO PARISYAN

THE X-GUARD

MARCELO GARCIA

MASTERING THE TWISTER

EDDIE BRAVO

MASTERING THE RUBBER GUARD

EDDIE BRAVO

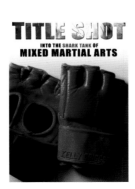

TITLE SHOT

KELLY CRIGGER

***MASTERING THE
RUBBER GUARD (DVD)***

EDDIE BRAVO

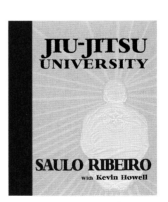

JIU-JITSU UNIVERSITY

SAULO RIBEIRO

ABOUT THE AUTHORS

ANTONIO RODRIGO NOGUEIRA, a black belt in Brazilian Jiu-Jitsu and judo, is the #1 ranked heavyweight mixed martial arts fighter in the world. He is the former RINGS King of Kings Tournament champion, former PRIDE heavyweight champion, and current UFC heavyweight champion.

GLEN CORDOZA is a professional Muay Thai kickboxer and mixed martial arts fighter. He is the author of ten books on the martial arts.

ERICH KRAUSS is a professional Muay Thai kickboxer who has lived and fought in Thailand. He has written for the New York Times and is the author of twenty books.